MW01115745

Unloving Me

A Memoir of a Girl from The Heights

Leydis D. De La Cruz

Copyright 2007

1

Unloving Me:
A Memoir of a Girl from The Heights

Table of Contents

Dedicated to God.
Thank you for guiding, protecting,
and for your providence throughout this journey.

Thank you to my inner child.
Your bravery is awe-inspiring.
Thank you for your courage, and, for remaining loving and
kind through it all.

Introduction

This is my journey, etched against the backdrop of a paperback. All my life, I have grappled with purpose, the journey, the destination, and the experiences that have shaped my life. At the center of the journey back to "soul-me", lies a series of relationships that thrust me into a quest around love, most importantly, love of self.

The author, Timothy Keller, in his book *The Meaning of Marriage* once wrote: "To be loved but not known is comforting but superficial. To be known and not loved is our greatest fear. But to be fully known and truly loved is, well, a lot like being loved by God".

Cultivating relationships has been - if anything, what most characterizes my journey. Ironically, my fears around love, which is what I have desired most, have made this one consuming journey.

Perhaps my beginnings shaped many of my beliefs about what love is and what it is not. I believe Keller speaks to the many superficial theories around what love feels like (attention, superficial connections); however, is that love? Is love based on how many people claim to love you but do not know you? They do not know the "naked you." The parts of you that are not revealed to the world. Do they love you despite your shortcomings? Do they love you as you are? Yet, the people who choose to love you despite your shortcomings and "emotional spikes" are the people who see the God in you.

My journey has been about seeing me the way God sees me, despite how my story started, the pain, the shame, the losses, and the experiences that nearly broke my back-sometimes my dignity and heart; I have an inalienable right to love.

What love would become or is made of could only be defined by the journey itself. The journey was a winding road composed of low and high peaks, where sometimes I lost, and sometimes I won. In fact, completing this book is one of my wins. Though the stories highlighted in this book were written in 2007, despite my best efforts, it was dawdled.

Something always seemed "unfinished." I understood then that it was about the journey itself..., so I waited.

This book has been an in-and-out project with no end date in sight. At the core was - trauma. Every time I worked on "perfecting" it; I would clutch my pearls as trauma wafted throughout my being as I attempted to edit the book. A reminder - that there was more internal work to be processed for the book to come together.

Furthermore, completing this book has reminded me that a lot in my life has been a constant wait. Waiting for better times, waiting for the storms to pass, waiting for those things I thought I deserved, just waiting until I waited no more.

At times, I felt as though there was a "spiritual garrote" around telling my story, preventing its completion. But there were no garrotes other than the paralyzing fear of getting naked before you, the reader. The fear of being seen as anything other than my "imperfect self", and the gut-wrenching shame around parts of my story. The waiting was keen on the process itself.

The permission to allow myself to heal and accept the parts of me that felt "unworthy" of my own story. The waiting was about healing my inner child and overcoming the waves of challenges life surely brings each one of us, which is nothing short of courageous work.

Abuse of any form, compounded trauma, and the choices we make leave an imprint on the soul. It is worth reclaiming our lives. It is the "calling" for each of us to live a life that is authentic to our souls. Neither our beginnings nor the trauma we experience define us. On the contrary, it strengthens our soul's core.

For you, beloved reader, I pray that your inner child is liberated through forgiveness, joy, and redemption if you haven't started your healing journey. I pray that the stories compiled in this book speak to the hell victims of abuse experience. Furthermore, that the glory is achieved through intentional healing.

Finally, I pray that you know you are infinite, powerful, loving, loved, and the world's most beautiful creation.

Thank you for picking up my book. Be and stay blessed

Disclaimer:
I have tried to recreate events, places, and conversations from my memories of them. To maintain their anonymity in some instances I have altered names of individuals and places described in this book.

Please note that this memoir contains some explicit or potentially triggering content around sexual and physical abuse.

People See What They Are

You see a frayed woman,
a window whose backdrop is dreary and faded.
You see a sullen woman full of misfortune,
deficient of adventures,
a damsel without a Don Quixote.

You see a woman full of longing,
lost in her grief,
in love with what little hope resides within,
a face dejected by life tragedies,
and eyes creased by the journey.

You see a dilapidated barricade,
a fruitless face,
a stance that has surrendered.
I assure you; you couldn't be more misguided!

I see a Mule,
A woman with inimitable depth,
A gait that challenges,
A gaze that flagellates,
Dressed in black to regain strength,
Dressed in red to calm the mourning of unconsciousness,
An edifice erected with bricks solely built by her.

Behind that window... There is life!
A Magnolia tree that blooms in March,
A verse that keeps on sowing,
A desire to be her own inspiration,
And a What? For those who wish to threaten her.

Her aroma is a perennial whiff of gardenias,
Perpetual is the desire she provokes in men,
I see a woman who loves herself,
I see feet firmly planted for the next voyage.

I see a fragile, tender, capable,
resolute, and anointed woman,
with a countenance as strong as graphite.

You cannot see her depth within your limitations,
I see her with eyes that know the real story.

7

I Let It All Go to Shit

I am just a girl from the Heights. Washington Heights that is. I am an immigrant girl in a place where almost everyone looked like me, many people spoke my language, and others spoke languages I did not understand. The Heights is the highest point in Northern Manhattan. A community full of vim and vigor. Loud music emanating from passing cars, busy streets like those back home, with buildings that were very tall for my small eight-year-old self. Streets that were not tree-lined, the heat smelled different than back home, so yes, I live in the Heights, but I am not of the Heights. I migrated from the Dominican Republic at the age of eight, but, by that age, my novela had been unfolding for some time. Frankly speaking, I didn't know what a novela was. Nor did I know I was a protagonist, and most definitely, did not know that there were unforeseen forces, and people trying to take the leading role away from me.

Like most stories of love, mine too, began with the love of my parents. Especially my mother. I fantasized about her. I remember how tall and beautiful she was. My mother always smelled like White Gardenias. New leather. Like new adventures. An aroma that would signal to me her impending arrival…

I was what you would call a precocious child, full of energy, with a point of view on social matters by the tender age of five. I was a know-it-all (some may argue - I still am). It made me look older. I was older, at least older than most girls. Most girls just got to play, but adults always wanted to talk and play with me. Too much.

I remember my childhood fondly; I remember laughing a lot. Doing childlike things, but I also remember feeling nostalgic, heavy inside, and preoccupied with things that children normally do not worry about.

For five years, I would be separated from my mother, and as my novela unfolded, the script of those five years would hunt me for the next three and a half decades. Making the number five a significant number in my life. It will be the number that pieced everything together in my journey.

It was April of 2020, there was supposed to be hope, and bountiful delights as spring made its way to the busy New York City streets. Tulips were blossoming, Magnolia trees were decorating the streets with iterations of pinks and lavenders, and Cherry Blossoms competing with the brightness of Daffodils.

Yet the hopeful spring evaded me, as I had arrived at a time when everything was supposed to make sense, but nothing did. Yes! I let it all go to shit. I heard every component of my existence shattered. I've had things fall apart before, but this time, the cracks of my humanity murmured in my ear as it broke into a million pieces; this time, it shattered in the deepest of silences, the way a prayer breaks down in the fifth dimension.

I heard the applause of all the versions of me that had previously died, joined by all the people "who loved me" but secretly hated me.

For the first time in my life, I had no job. Jobless in the middle of a global pandemic, the world in turmoil, and the smell of death engulfing the globe. International protests reverberated so loudly it peered through the planet's soul; social justice on the scale, the world had gone to shit, and I went with it.

Forty-three years old, 200lbs (not cute, I'm 5 '2,) jobless, loveless, depressed, and for the first time in my life..., I was okay with being all these things, or so I told myself.

It dawned on me, that I managed to plow through trauma by keeping busy all my life, and never having the time to just sit with my shit. It occurred to me that things falling apart may be a blessing in disguise. To finally allow myself to sit in it long enough to know how bad it smelled. To have the time to grieve all my losses, to grieve the versions of me that died without care, without aid, a proper burial, and frankly, without my permission!

I now had the time to look at my life through the lens of intentionality. These men, how did they get to shape me without my consent? Relationships? I failed at every relationship I have ever had, the biggest of them all..., the relationship with myself.

I realized I had been a mechanical robot powering through life simply taking orders. Taking orders from family, employers, friends, men, God, and whatever stranger summoned me to help them.

In April 2020, I ascertained that I had no autonomy. It was embarrassing to admit to my soul that I had lied to everyone about who I was; more troublesome, I had lied to myself.

Sitting in my dining room, meditating on the infamous "Footprints" hanging on my white wall as a Black Jesus carried me in his arms (I'd like to think that it's me he's carrying in his arms,) when I decided that I was going to 'Sit in My Shit'! "You take care of me through this," I said to Black Jesus. And into hermit mode I went.

How The Shit Started

Happy Chaos has surrounded me from early on; it makes sense - I was born on Christmas day. The first girl to be delivered at La Altagracia Centro de Maternidad that midnight (not sure how happy that made my mother,) but here I was! And she received a basket for bringing me into this world; *I am, the gift that keeps on giving.*

Born on Jesus's day according to the Catholic Faith, and to everyone's surprise, I was born with two bottom teeth or natal teeth (I am sure everyone thought I was the Antichrist incarnate). *Happy chaos!*

Think about it: Dominican Republic, in 1976, a baby born with two teeth was an anomaly. My mother says that people were hesitant to hold me, fearing my teeth were a bad omen..., it makes sense; relating to people was hard for me from day one!

Here I am, with exceptional chaos since birth, born on one of the holiest and happiest days of the Catholic faith, given a name that would later become royalty (but we know the ending of those two iconic figures), and two bottom teeth! What can go wrong?

My life as I remember it begins at three years of age, when like so many families throughout the world, my mother migrated to the United States in search of a better future for me and my siblings.

I was three, and I remember that moment like it was yesterday. I remember holding onto my mother's legs for dear life, as if intrinsically knowing that my life - would never be the same if she left. I remember crying hysterically, begging her not to leave. Not to leave me alone. I was scared.

My mom looked at me and told me she'd be back for me and to take care of my sister. "El grande cuida al chiquito." So, when we (my sister and I) were sent to an All-girls boarding school staffed by nuns, it was my responsibility to ensure that my three-year-old self cared after my two-year-old sister.

In many Latino cultures, we teach our children responsibility. We teach our children to care for their sibling(s) and to protect and guide the younger ones..., a commendable life lesson. I think placing such a burden on a small child, sets them up to be adults who struggle with being responsible for themselves, launching them into very dangerous emotional tug of wars as adults.

Not too long after, we left the boarding school to a family member's house. Yeah, we moved a lot, quite a lot. It felt as though, I could not last very long at any place, or be welcomed for long stays. Perhaps it's the reason I love the act of moving. Perhaps it's because, by eight years old, I had lived in various places. Yet, the ritual of picking up and starting anew is refreshing and hopeful one for me, (something that would seep into my adult life as I deal with "projects").

Contradictory perhaps (do you know me?), as freeing as the act of moving is, I love stability. Don't think I've known it, I have attempted to have it in every area of my life, and very possibly have failed in each one. Maybe it's too soon to tell.

There are many dangers when families are separated. To the growing child, for example, not having the ability to hug their parent, get a kiss, or to even be scolded for misbehaving is already a disadvantage. That child does not understand that mom and dad have left the country to give them a better life. That child knows that other children have parents at home, and they don't. That child is already at an emotional disadvantage because those cues, learned behaviors, or how relationships are formed are not there. The concepts of protection, loyalty, love, and boundaries have all been mired by a sense of displacement, abandonment, nomadism, instability, and other socio and psychological issues that would expand as the child grows into an adult battling with these issues. There's a break in the family unit. This is not a disclaimer, nor a position on immigration. These are things that happen when children and parents are separated.

Five years would forever define my history, it's how long I was separated from my mother. Five years and my life would never be the same. Perhaps, in the context of this vast universe, five years is relatively nothing. It takes five years for mango and papaya trees to produce its fruit. But for little girls, five years is too long to be away from their mother.
Those five years would define how I weaved throughout life. My relationships with men, with God, and friendships. Most importantly, it would forever change my relationship with myself.
The impact of those five years away from my parents has never made more sense to me than now that I have chosen to let everything go to shit. I was scared, and terrified (more than when I was a child). As a child, I could escape my reality through my imagination, but, that little girl died long ago.
The imposed COVID-19 lockdown forced me to sit with 40 years of trauma, pain, a deep sense of failure, and loss. It compelled me to sit with the one person I hated and loved

the most... Me! Of course, That 'ME' also included all the failed relationships I had with men.

Part of the immigrant experience for many families is that children are often left to the care of other family members, while the parents work overseas to eventually reunite the family. During those five years my siblings and I, moved around quite a bit. Every move brought about its happy chaos, joys, and challenges.

I grew up in a large family. Too big! Surrounded by lots of cousins, aunts, uncles, and my grandparents. With every home a different accommodation. Different rules of acceptable behavior, shared resources, and so on.

The first home I remember being at was with an older paternal cousin. I remember that it was a modest home. I don't necessarily remember the interior layout or decoration of the house. Ingrained in me, however, was the kitchen and the adjacent cement sink. Most homes in the Dominican Republic have an outdoor cement sink adjacent to the kitchen. This sink is where many of the larger items are cleansed and used to wash clothes.

I remember that sink so vividly because it would always leak graywater, and that is also where my eldest cousin would feed me whenever I misbehaved; that greywater would drip onto my plate. I still remember the plinking, dripping sound of dirty water falling onto my plate. I don't think she did it out of malice, but rather from a place of frustration, and feeling overwhelmed by the responsibility of caring for young children. I am unsure how old she was then, but I'm sure she didn't even reach her mid-twenties.

This type of punishment, and others throughout my childhood, created an apathy for food in me, like the time "meat - got me beat!"

It was noon, lunchtime in my country. After Sunday mass, "El Almuerzo" is one of the most sacred, and revered time in the country…, Dominicans value their "almuerzo" time. The family gathered around the table to enjoy mangu with stewed chicken (a delicacy in my eyes coming from the Internado). My stomach was filled with joyous expectation,

16

as this was one of my favorite dishes growing up. I was savoring every bite; the way the gooey and buttery mashed plantain melted in my mouth as the sauce from the stew chicken nuzzled my throat. I always left my meat for last as I enjoyed chewing on the bone. There was a knock at the door. I didn't care about the knock; I had my favorite dish before me, and no door knock would disrupt my joyous expectation.

A man I don't remember (perhaps I don't care to remember his features, scent, or name) came to visit at the most sacred time in our country. The *man I don't care to remember* about, was invited to sit at the family table. I am not sure if there was enough food for him to have been invited to the table, but my dear uncle instructed me to give up my meat to this intruder and 'meat stealer,' all for politeness, which came at my expense!

In my country, it is frowned upon to arrive at anyone's house at noon time because everyone understands families are gathered for lunch and understand the sacredness of family time. Did no one tell this man about customs or principles? Why was he there disrupting my joyous expectations? True to my nature, I said "No." My uncle commanded me to hand over the meat for a second time. I gave him a definite "No." My uncle took my "insubordination" as disrespect.

My dear political uncle, who at the time seemed like seven feet tall to whatever inches tall I was at four years old, snatched me from the table, dragged me to the bathroom, and into the tub I went. As the cold water splashed on my small frame, he struck my body with his thick leather belt in retribution for my "insolence" and "disobedience."

I took the beating but ate my meat!

It was the principle of it all, and *perhaps, on a subconscious level, this is the reason why I have been a vegetarian for two and half decades... Because "meat gets you beat!"*

17

I could not understand why the adults around that table didn't give up their meat. Why, of all the people sitting at that table, was I chosen to give up my food? More infuriating is: Why are children being asked to give up their food for un lambón?

These types of experiences shaped my relationship with food. Thankfully, I didn't develop any mental food disorders, but it's the beginning of maladaptive behaviors related to self-care as an adult. I ate if I felt hungry, but food has never been of the essence for me... "Man does not live by bread alone, but on every word that proceeds from the mouth of God." Matthew 4:4.

Many of our moves were sudden and without an explanation (A los muchachos no se le da explicaciones, ¡nada!) and one blindly follows orders,) and off we were to an Internado de Monjas (An all-girls boarding school run by nuns).

My cousin was saintly compared to these nuns - God; those nuns were mean spirited! Not all of them, many of them. They were rigid and ungodly. One had to follow the rules because if not, severe punishments would follow to atone for the sin (breathing was a sin,) i.e., if a child wet the bed, they would take out the cot and have the child kneel on rice in the blazing sun facing the mattress until it dried. If you misspoke, you would not eat. Not that I cared about the food because it was undesirable; those nuns were the Forrest Gump of Arenque (Herring). Herring was served almost daily (Locrio de Arenque, Arenque guisado con plátanos, Arenque con huevo frito). Herring was served so often that a fight would ensue whenever meat was served.

God always sends good people in to help and protect us. While in boarding school, Sister Tere was my angel on earth. She was the protector, the nun who would tell us to get up from kneeling on rice when the other nuns were not watching. Sister Tere would give advice and ways to dodge severe punishment. She taught me how to make Sacramental bread or "Eucharist" (given to parishioners during the Catholic mass). Her love - was my saving grace. I remember her kindness, hugs, and devotion to all the girls at that school.
Besides Sister Tere, the only good thing about being in that Internado was being picked up by my paternal grandfather every other weekend. When he picked my sister and me up, my day brightened, as any respite from those nuns was a blessing.

19

My paternal grandfather is the first man I loved (I don't remember much about my father at this age since he emigrated to the U.S., before my mother,) but my Papa Melanio was my king, and I loved him more than life itself. In between the moving, and the apparent mischievousness, there was laughter, there were games, and there was my beloved grandfather Melanio. I remember him as my protector. I think he's the only man who ever truly protected and loved me without variants, without exchanges, without force.

Papa was tall and regal, reminding me of the Caciques from our Taino ancestry. His skin was the most beautiful color I had seen, as if the sunset and sunrise fused together, and created a color just for him. Papa Melanio had a pronounced nose, big ears, and a full head of gray hair. He was funny and loving and smelled like tobacco leaves and spring. His scent invades me when I'm distressed, almost as if telling me, "Don't be afraid. I'm here with you."

My abuelo Melanio was a Tabaquero, and much of our time together consisted of sitting around the kitchen table, helping him sort through and pick apart tobacco leaves that he would then roll into cigars. He would share old tales and joke around as we worked on the leaves.

His speech was soft. I don't remember his voice anymore, but I remember how soothing it felt to me, like the calmness that looking at a body of water and trees invokes in me.

Our nights culminated with a recap of the previous week at the Internado, where he would ask: if my sister and I were being "good" and whatever else grandparents discuss with their grandchildren. It was so refreshing to spend time with my abuelo, and I remember our time filled with much joy, laughter, and love.

I'm unsure as to why he stopped picking up my sister and me from the Internado, but like most men in my life, he vanished. It would be years before I found out that he had transitioned. I don't recall when he died, nor what year he died, or if I went to his funeral. He was just gone. No explanation, no goodbyes, nada, as if he never existed. As if his hugs were a fabrication of my mind which felt so real; those hugs which even in my adulthood I reminisced about when solitude was my only visitor.

I remember my grandfather's love when older men would want to play with me because I knew that my grandfather did not play like that.

All those years I did not see my abuelo Melanio, I thought I had done something wrong, and that he did not want to see me anymore. The pattern *of not explaining things to me* left me with a thousand questions, guilt, and a deep sense of abandonment. Although I never saw him again, my Papa Melanio stayed present throughout my life. He visits me in dreams to give me warnings and messages. I didn't understand it as a child, but that spiritual connection with my grandfather was my introduction to the ethereal, the esoteric, and the belief that our departed never leave us. They are always with us -in us. Even as a child, I remember talking to him as if he had never left (I speak to the dead more than the living. I find them safer.)

Following the Internado, we moved in with more family members before reuniting with my mother. The last place we settled in was a small and modest one-bedroom house shared with eight people. For the most part, this home was a happy one. There was no physical violence, we ate well, and we got to play outdoors after school. Nevertheless, my disdain for nighttime came during this period of my life. Of all the places I lived as a child, this was the most violent towards my spirit.

I detested nighttime at this place; as beautiful as the sunset was, with its landing over the avocado trees, it was a reminder that nightfall would follow. When the sun set, I had to face a demon. A human flesh demon, with no horns, with no red skin, and no tale demon. My little heart trembled when the dark sky descended because when the lights went out, El Cuco came out to visit me. El Cuco is a monster-traditionally used in Latino homes to scare or intimidate children.

El Cuco came almost every night, but not the four-legged Cuco who crawled through the streets of La Feria, and of whom I was terrified of. Street Cuco had cerebellar hypoplasia, a deformity that causes an imbalance in the body, and to adapt, quadrupedalism or locomotion (walking on hands and feet) is developed. I was terrified of Cuco because adults use people's deformities to scare children, but this Cuco did not harm me. Four-legged Cuco was no match to El Cuco who visited me at night.

I was unsure what was happening to me at night or why my uncle would put his mouth on my vagina until I urinated. I knew I didn't like it. I felt dirty, and as if I was a bad girl. I suffered from headaches often, depleted of energy most days. I surmise that it was a physiological response to the internal turmoil I was enduring.

The abuse continued for a long time until one day I visited my next-door neighbor, whom I consider an earth angel sent to stop the sexual abuse. I enjoyed visiting with

Dilcia; she and her brothers who were kind and loving towards me. I felt safe in their home.

On one of those visits, Dilcia noticed that I consistently suffered headaches and asked why I had recurring headaches. She asked a series of questions about nutrition, sleep, and violence. She wondered if someone was hurting me. I did not respond to the "hurt" question because, at that time, I did not understand that what my uncle was doing was considered 'hurting me,' and since no one was physically hurting me with a belt, I didn't associate the words.

She asked if someone was touching me inappropriately and gave examples of what inappropriately meant. I confessed to her what was happening to me most nights and that I didn't like nighttime. She asked if I had shared this before, and I replied, "No." She suggested that the next time Cuco attempted to molest me - to scream.

I followed suit, and one of those nights, I woke up to his mouth on my vagina and screamed. El Cuco quickly moved so no one noticed. He waited and tried it again. This time, I screamed louder, waking my Uncle Tony, and catching Cuco in the act.

Tio Tony never addressed the incident nor asked if I was okay. All I know is that the pedophile was gone, and nighttime was not as scary. I never quite had a normal sleep for fear that Cuco would return, and I'd wake up to his filthy mouth on me.

I also told my aunt about it, to which she replied, "You play with boys too much."

I used to dream of my mother, I wanted to be like her a lot.
I missed her a lot, especially when adults wanted to play, when the nuns were being harsh, or when they would make my three-year-old sister kneel on rice in the scorching sun until her mattress dried from wetting it the previous night. I missed my mom, when the nuns fed us the same food every day of the week, or when food was taken away as punishment. Or when the children would say that "my mom did not love me." I knew it wasn't true, but, when I missed her, and she wouldn't come, I used to ask God, if it was true that she "did not love me?"

Then out of thin air, and as if she heard my cry, my mom would appear. It became apparent, that every time my mom came, something bad had happened. Very bad.

The "very bad visit" was usually related to an emergency pertaining my siblings and me. For example, the time my sister split her forehead open in the Internado after jumping from a stack of cots my peers and I piled together pretending we could fly. It was a frightening experience. The blood, my little sister not moving, and in my head, I heard my mom asking me "How did you let this happen, you're supposed to take care of your sister?" I think that it was the first time the word "responsibility" clicked for me, and how much of a "failure" I was for not being a responsible sister. Every time, I look at my sister's forehead and see the scar which healed as a 'cross' (a memento of sorts from the nun's bad stitch work) I am reminded of "responsibility". Not only were those nuns mean, but also had poor sowing skills.

Then there was the time my second eldest brother got into an accident after missing the landing from a speeding truck. There she was again, my mom, with her statuesque beauty, her new leather smell, her long frame, that radiant smile, and her tired gleaming eyes to the rescue.

My Mom looked stunning each time I saw her. I glean that all children find their mother to be the most beautiful woman they know. Her beautiful brown skin, wavy

24

black hair, and coiffure were decorated with the most immaculate and angelic smile I had ever seen; perhaps, because she had perfectly aligned white teeth which made her smile perfection- if perfection knew itself. My mother was tall, bony, and smoked Virginia Slims as if her life depended on it.

I still remember how she held cigarettes in her hands, as if she jumped out of a magazine with her fashion-forward style, looking gorgeous, calm, graceful, and collected. Most impressive was her walk; her step was gracious and poised as if time was rushing her, but she defied it. My mom was the most beautiful woman I had ever seen.

Mom never announced her visits; instinctively, I knew through dreams, or the scent of brand-new leather would invade my senses days before her visit, which signaled to me that her visit was near. It was a relief to see her. I didn't care what the reason for my mom's visit was, I just expected that with each emergency or holiday, she would say: "I'm staying or enough..., we are all leaving now"! But it wouldn't happen for some time.

Every time she left; I wondered if she knew what was happening to me. Did she know what was happening to me, and thought that like my aunt "I played too much with boys?" Did the adults not tell her? Who were they protecting?

Reunited, But It Doesn't Feel So Good

I reunited with my mother in Washington Heights, New York City, which is in the Northern section of Upper Manhattan, in the summer of 1985. The experience was exciting, overwhelming, and magical. I first thought about my height when I saw a mountain of skyscrapers.

New York City's air and scent engrossed my soul when my feet landed. I was only eight years old but immediately fell in love with it. The city's vibrancy felt unique, as though the streets released electrical discharges with each majestic architecture.

The sounds emanating from cars playing music I didn't understand, but my soul did. The streets had a beat like none I had experienced, as if the asphalt were playing music with each person's step; and with every step, the thump got louder and louder.

Washington Heights gave me the same feeling. It was the first time I had seen that many people at once in the street. Even La Calle Duarte felt less transited than Washington Heights did. The Heights was loud, enthusiastic, and vibrant! Seeing fire pumps gushing water onto children playing perplexed me, for back home, we had to walk some distance to a well to draw and carry water for daily use. I felt rich in a way.

We lived on 181st Street and Wadsworth, and therefore, we were at the center of all the action. 181st Street was busy because it homed major stores such as Woolworth, Wertheimer's, but also the George Washington Bridge, the Cross Bronx Bridge, in addition to being a transportation hub to other parts of the city.

Our building covered the entire block; therefore, everyone knew each other. The building was ethnically diverse hence, I grew up with Polish, Greeks, Puerto Ricans, Cubans, Jewish, Mexicans, and Irish people, which exposed me to many cultures and traditions at a young age.

My mother had remarried by the time we reunited, which was a bit confusing because no one informed me that my parents had divorced, then again, 'a los muchachos no se les da explicaciones.' While back home in the D.R., I did occasionally speak to a man with a strange accent who spoke fast, but I was too young to understand the concept of a stepfather.

My stepfather, who is of Cuban descent, has been an enigmatic figure in my life. He's bright, fun, whimsical, and rigid. True to his Gemini Sun, he's not to be boxed in any category. He provided for us and was an overprotective Dad. People knew not to mess with him or his family.

The summer of 1985 was exhilaratingly fun: exploring the scent of New York City, going to the beach, the amusement parks, and family outings. It was a different kind of fun from the Dominican Republic. Back home, childhood fun was an interpersonal experience. For instance, if the lights were to go out (electrical grid powers off. This was one of the things I loved about NYC, there was always light), all the children would gather on the street and play childhood games like La Gallina, Coronel Pasando Lista, Mariquita Abusadora, and You're Tag. During daylight, we were just outside or playing Jacks. Conversely, in the U.S., fun was going to places and not relating to other children as I did back home. Perhaps because my parents were strict, unlike back home, I was not allowed to hang outdoors or in front of the building like most kids I saw through the window.

The best part of being reunited was being around my mother at last. However, I always sensed that she was constantly tense. The air in the house was taut. Rigid. I'm not sure if the five years away from me changed her - how it changed me, but it seemed as if she was perpetually preoccupied—the house draped in secrecy and uncomfortable silence. I couldn't voice out certain things, bring up my biological father's name at home, or speak up if

27

I felt displeased. Everything was a secret (I had so many already). It felt like *discomfort* was the main dish served during supper, and you just had to eat it up.

Sometimes, the home was so joyous, but at times, no one spoke to one another..., complete and utter silence. Almost as if uttering a word would burst into the most explosive event. The environment fluctuated from joyous, solemn, or dead silent. The most extravagant parties would take place, and the next day, everyone acted as if we were all strangers in a land where everyone knew each other but didn't quite like each other.

This is where I developed my hyper-vigilance, the constant need to assess the energy of a room to observe and absorb the temperature of its player to proceed accordingly. A regular self-monitoring: Am I safe? Is it safe to speak? Is it safe to be me? Can I laugh now? I shouldn't say that because it will cause this. Incessantly regulating my behavior through internal dialogue and mapping out the exits should I have to run. I have been, for the most part, in a constant state of heightened anticipatory planning.

Two years had not gone by when my mom "deported" my sister and me back to the D.R. (Dominicans have their immigration process.) There is no explanation; you and your sister are going to the D.R. Ten-year-old me translated this as; you must leave because you are too much of a "rebellious child." I spoke back, and when something did not make sense, I challenged the status quo. Ten-year-old me felt like a nuisance to my mom, and she didn't want me around anymore.

I lived with my maternal grandparents during those two years in the Dominican Republic. My Mom had just purchased a beautiful home for my grandparents, where close to fifteen family members lived. The house was busy, clamorous, and, for the most part, very joyful.

The house was in the Capital of Santo Domingo, yet it felt like we were in the Campo since it was as green as the Conucos in the countryside. I woke up to the smell of mango, coconut, cherry, Limoncillos, Soursop, avocado trees, and all the other trees planted in that house. We also did a bit of poultry farming for domestic consumption. The back portion of the house had a colossal straw gazebo lounge area where most family celebrations would occur.

I spent my days climbing trees after school and playing outdoors with my cousins and aunts (who were a year or a few apart from me.)

I became a "Señorita" during this time, and true to everything in my life, no one explained what was happening to me. Mother received the "Leydis is a señorita phone call," and the house celebrated the grand news that I had begun menstruating. I got the lecture on "comportate como señorita," but not what to do with my bleeding vagina or why my vagina was bleeding at all. Thankfully, my next-door neighbor understood my confusion, spoke to me, and later bought me a book on what was happening to me, and what I should expect every month. Happy chaos!

While I missed my mom dearly, spending time with my grandmother, Mama Juanita, and Great-Grandmother, Mama Nena- two influential females in my life was a decent trade-off. My Mama Juanita was the sweetest woman I have ever met (if sugar can be a person, it was her!). There was a purity about her I have yet to experience since. She was soft-spoken, poised, and possessed a quiet strength that was powerful to witness. Mama Juanita resolved everything with patience, a smile, and love. I surmise that birthing fifteen children gives you a level of patience only attained by truly divine individuals.

I characterize Mama's warm smile as a *hopeful and gleeful poem that disregards all of life's suffering for the possibility of brighter days.*

She didn't take anything too seriously, making her everyone's ally. She possessed an unshakable faith that taught me to trust the unseen more than my circumstances. Mama was the embodiment of gratitude. She gave 'thanks' for everything. Mama Juanita taught me that love, a smile, and a good disposition get you along farther in life. It's hard to fight someone who smiles, speaks life into you, and laughs at your perceived "bad behavior."

Then, there was my Mama Nena. No mother-daughter duo could ever be so different; if Juanita was Venus, Mama Nena was Mars. She was fiery but impartial, proud but humble, outspoken, loving, and kind. When Mama Nena spoke, the entire house listened (trembled,) almost as if the whole place was summoned for the transgressions of the one sinner.

Mama Nena commanded respect and was a no-nonsense kind of person. She usually wore her hair in braids and only wore white or brown clothing (a promise she made or something like that.) While she was in and out throughout my two-year stay, Mama Nena taught me many lessons I carried into adulthood. She recited stories as she combed my hair at night, and all these stories had subliminal messages about self-empowerment, agency, authenticity, and showing up for yourself as a woman in the world. She was ahead of her time as I reflected on her. I surmise that Mama Juanita wanted her strength, and Mama Nena often wondered what "a soft woman" was like.

The incongruity between these two women taught me early on that: A woman can be both sweet and strong. Embody both feminine (nurturing energy) and masculine (strength and protective side). While my grandmothers relied more on one aspect of their energies (feminine or masculine), they could summon them as needed because it was part of their core. The way each achieved it - varied, but it was right. One chose softness, and the other one operated from sternness. Nonetheless, those combined energies were an excellent example for me growing up.

They shaped my mother and me in the process. My Mana Nena was there when I was born, and according to my mother, because I was born sickly and with two teeth, people feared being around or holding me. Only Mana Nena held me because she wasn't afraid of my two teeth or sickly demeanor. That's the thing: Bonds don't care about illness nor fear it. Bonds are built on love because love is the only thing that overcomes fear. So, as the world refused to embrace me because of the way I looked, my Mama Nena embraced me as if I was the most precious gem she ever held in her arms. She and my mother's love nursed me back to health.

I was twelve years old when I returned to Washington Heights from my two-year deportation to reunite with my mother once more. The home environment was still tense, and school became my haven. I loved going to school because, during that time, I felt free. I thought I could be loud and speak up without getting punished for having a different perspective than my parents or siblings.

I attended I.S. 143 located between Audubon and Amsterdam to complete the 8th grade. I was placed in a monolingual class because I spoke enough conversational English, but the reality is that I lost what little English I learned during my two-year deportation. It was one of the most challenging years of my academic life! My classmates constantly made fun of me because of my accent. I didn't understand the class material because I was not fluent in English. I began feeling simple-minded, inadequate, and a failure, but I was not a dumb child; I skipped grades in elementary school because I was too bright, which frustrated me even more.

The girls were mean! I was twelve with the body of an 18-year-old. I mean, I had Salma Hayek's large breasts at twelve and a body that attracted all the wrong attention. I had a charisma that brought all the boys towards me, and the girls did not like that. Since my life has always been happy chaos, for some reason, my enemies always became my friends. I'm not sure if it's the "have your friends close, and your enemies closer" type of deal, but for me, so long as they didn't put their hands on me, what they thought of me did not matter. Half the time, I did not understand what they were saying due to my limited English..., but my spirit did.

I discovered Hip-Hop during this time, and much like New York City and Washington Heights, I instantly fell in love with it, which is how I learned English. There was something about the sound and lyrics I could not fully understand with my limited English, but it resonated and enthralled my spirit.

The Hip-Hop I grew up with spoke to injustice; that is what resonated with my soul. I recognized it without understanding what it was, but it spoke to a part of me that wanted the same thing..., justice! I was seeking justice and found it in those lyrics. I would go home and play hip-hop songs on my Walkman (a cassette player with headphones that allowed listening to music as you walked) and replayed the song until I learned to annunciate the lyrics (I am sure that what the artist was saying was not what came out of my mouth- but I tried). I did this with every hip-hop song that dropped in 1989.

While I loved hip-hop and still do, I know that subconsciously, I was trying to fit in. To not be made fun of because of my accent, while regarding who I was: a Dominican immigrant, trying to speak two languages, trying to be young, and trying to find my voice in the vast ether of American life.

I entered George Washington High School (G-dubs) at age of twelve. It was massive. It felt as big as La Calle Duarte on a Saturday afternoon with so many bodies attending that school. High School was my favorite academic experience and was filled with happy chaos.

G-Dubs was one electrifying building with enough adrenaline to fuel a dead man's body back to life. The energies, the potential, the commitment of those teachers, the security officers; that building contained all the politicians, the engineers, the dancers, and the baseball superstars of the future everything!

G-Dubs was a racially and ethnically charged building. The Blacks did not like Dominicans. The American-born Dominicans did not like the newly arrived Dominicans, and everyone hated the Metal and Goth kids.

I got the nickname "Mike Tyson" (before the infamous "ear bite" fight) by this point. I never looked for trouble, but people knew not to mess with me. The first week of school, a Weightlifting sophomore student threw a fruit cup at me, a hazing of sorts, except that I wasn't any regular Freshman. I jumped from across the cafeteria lunch table, put him in a headlock, and threw as many punches to his face as I could. I am unsure if I won the fight, but the entire school learned that day that I was not the one to mess with.

I used to get requests from many of the recently arrived Dominican girls to intercede on their behalf from the Dominican American-born girls who were bullying them. It was common for the Dominican-born girls to wait for the newly arrived students after school. They would strip these poor girls of their clothes during the winter months in front of the students/people hanging out in front of the school as the 3:00 p.m. bell rang. When I say strip, I mean strip them down to their socks in frigid temperatures, including snow.

While for them, it was pure fun to ridicule these timid, afraid, and vulnerable girls, for me, it was unjust and evil. I never confronted them intending to fight on their behalf, but I used my reputation to stop what we now call "bullying." If the mediation got messy, I would fight the bullies, and ultimately, the bullying of those girls would stop (I began my activism at an early age). These "intercession requests" extended outside the wall of G-dubs.

I was a well-liked lone wolf in High School; I enjoyed knowing many people but basked even more on not needing clicks to get through the day.

After school, my friends and I would walk around the community or visit the dead. Yes, my friends and I had this morbid obsession with walking into Rivera or Ortiz Funeral homes to console the family and friends of the deceased (this was in the '90s and way before *"The Hangover."*) We struck up conversations, asked for the cause of death, hugged, and depending on the story - sometimes cried with the family and friends at the wakes.
The guests often confused us for the deceased's family members or friends.

"Ah, tu no eres la hija de Fulanito?"

"Si" was always our answer.

Perhaps it was insensitive, as I reflected, but in our teenagers' minds, we didn't think we were offending or hurting anyone by that; to the contrary, we saw it as supporting people in need (I know. Delusional!)

High School was fun, but going home wasn't, and by God's grace, I found Alianza Dominicana or Alianza Dominicana found me. Happy Chaos!

Alianza Dominicana, Inc.

Alianza Dominicana, Inc., was the largest not-for-profit organization serving the Northern Manhattan area and later the Bronx. It provided a wide range of social services to families and youth.

I ended up in the A.I.D.P (Attendance Improvement Drop-Out Program), designed to help students at risk of dropping out due to poor academic performance and attendance. Their office was located on the fourth floor of G-Dubs and staffed with case managers who helped at-risk youth get back on track to graduation. The staff was caring, engaged, and committed to ensuring that every young person who entered through their threshold had a fair chance at graduation.

The team organized activities to reward students for improved attendance and grades. Due to their financial status, the A.I.D.P program was the only ticket for many youths to explore the city and enjoy recreational activities, such as museums, amusement parks, Broadway plays, etc. We often dismiss how influential this programming can be in underserved or marginalized communities, especially its impact on youth. Access to tutoring services, SAT practices, and counseling services may be financially impossible for many low-income youths.

Moreover, the opportunity and exposure to experiences that expand and broaden their horizon to a bigger world is indisputably the inflection point for many low-income youths who attend these programs. Being exposed to art shows and retreats outside their neighborhoods, let alone their city provides young people a peek into the possibility that they, too, have an escape route if they choose.

It teaches them about redemption in a way, with the message that life offers opportunities to course-correct the path. Programs like A.I.D.P. are vital because they celebrate progress, and youth are seldom celebrated or acknowledged for improvement.

After school, I would go to the Alianza After-School Program at a storefront office on 176th Street and Amsterdam. It would become the beginning of what I know is part of my life's purpose - 'Service' and the catalyst to my inner child healing. It was the first time I saw an agency led by Dominican leaders, who spoke my language, looked like me, and where grassroots efforts would change the landscape of the Washington Heights community.

I joined the agency's folkloric dance group, and through this activity, I began learning about the African influence in Dominican music, heritage, and culture. I performed in the Dominican parades, City Hall, and Jacob Javits.; I consider the friendships I made through the dance group extended family members, dating back more than thirty years.

Shortly after joining the dance group, I became involved in The Core Group- a youth program that provided a platform for young people to discuss home life, school, and social issues affecting them. For the first time in my life, I knew I was not the only one experiencing challenge and with the core belief that, as a society, we had a problem and should do something about it. I felt empowered to have an opinion and have adults listen to them.

Washington Heights of the '80s and '90s looked very different from today's gentrified version. Two versions of Washington Heights existed, divided between the West of Broadway where most White people lived, and East of Broadway where Dominicans and minorities lived). East of Broadway was vibrant, from culinary diversity, access to goods, and nightlife. The community's east side had Village Alegre, a Cuban family-owned restaurant with the most exquisite food and ice cream. Secretly, the restaurant's patrons visited to witness the iconic and explosive meltdowns of Doña Carmen as she and her kids berated her loving and bashful husband, Manolo. I believe all the patrons waited for the day Manolo snapped to no avail. I don't think he had it in him; he reminded me a lot of my Mama Juanita, just too gentle of a soul, and a laugh-it-off attitude.

El Baturro was another Cuban-owned restaurant located on 184th and St. Nicholas. My family and I visited here often. I have great memories of the place, some being my Stepdad's grand displays of love for my mom as he would get on his knees and profess his love for my mom while dancing.

Margot's restaurant, known as La Reina del Con-Con, was a Dominican-owned restaurant popularized for the taste of 'home' in her food.

There were shops like Loco-Loco where you could find swimming wear in the wintertime and other goods. East of Broadway had it all. Seldom did its residents need to leave the community to find goods or services.

West of Broadway had McDonald's, the Coliseum, the majestic Cloisters, the Hudson River side, and the 181st Movie Theater. The first movie I saw on the big screen was in that theater. I will never forget the experience of sitting in a massive black room watching movies I didn't understand but feeling as if I did. While West of Broadway had the Coliseum, East of Broadway had the United Palace and the Audubon Ballroom, where the transcendent Human Rights Activist Malcolm X was assassinated.

East of Broadway had more culinary diversity than its counterpart. It had more accessibility and vibrancy, but it also had more problems.

West of Broadway had cleaner streets with garbage receptacles on every other block. East of Broadway didn't. Residents walked with trash in their hands for blocks until they could find a receptacle to dispose of their garbage; others would just throw it on the street or sidewalks.

West of Broadway was quiet, East of Broadway was cacophonous. The most striking difference between the

West and East of Broadway was the greenspaces (parks or playgrounds). For example, West of Broadway had gardens with various games on the playground area and clean and well-kept parks. The parks on East of Broadway were filled with crack vials, not as well kept, and contained little game variety for children to play in, making it dangerous for families to spend quality time and enjoy the beauty of the Heights.

Alianza Dominicana was instrumental in the Washington Heights we see today. One of the first activities I was involved in through the Core Group was a park beautification project. One by one, the agency began restoring the parks located East of Broadway area so that families can enjoy the green spaces in the community. To the teenager in me, that experience taught me about the collective good, and that small groups of people can affect change at the macro level if we unite.

The late Commissioner of Youth Services, Richard Murphy, under the late Mayor David Dinkins's administration, visited several Community-Based Organizations (CBOs) throughout New York City to assess the needs of young people. Alianza Dominicana's Youth Core Group had the opportunity to meet with the late Commissioner about creating the perfect center for youth and what that space would look like. The sum of all these meetings birthed the first ten Beacon Programs across New York City. In the summer of 1991, Alianza Dominicana, Inc., La Plaza Beacon Program housed inside I.S. 143 Junior High School opened its doors to hundreds of Washington Heights/Inwood youths.

The Beacon Program model utilizes school buildings in underserved communities, which are traditionally unoccupied after 3:00 p.m., a time when young people are most susceptible to getting into trouble (idle hands, devil's playground,) to provide a wide range of social, educational, and recreational services to youth and the community at large between 3:00-10:00 p.m. It was a monumental time for young people across the city, forever changing the lives of hundreds of thousands of youths by engaging them through after-school programming.

The Beacons became a haven of expression while partaking in arts, recreational activities, tutoring, dance, counseling, activism, etc. It also provided youth employment opportunities by hiring them as tutors and instructors to children and youth in those programs.

Beacon Programs were transformative on so many levels. Many young people like me contributed to our households' economies through the entrepreneurial opportunities afforded by Alianza. Young people who otherwise would depend on their parents for the day-to-day economic exchange were now direct contributors to their homes and the community at large. I was spending my money in all the mom-and-Pop stores in the community, the movie theater, the Bodegas, and, yes, Loco-Loco like everyone else.

The Beacons also became a resource hub for adults as well. We provided ESL, arts, and citizenship classes, GED, and a place where families would receive counseling, mental health services, etc.

La Plaza Beacon Program would become the epicenter and refuge for youth and adults caught in the middle of the '92 riots, spawned by the murder of Kiko Garcia, who was shot in the back by a police officer. The tension between local youths and police officers had been brewing for months before Garcia's murder, and his death was the catalyst for the protest.

As news came in of the riots, La Plaza remained open until 2:00 a.m., holding young people and adults indoors until deemed safe to return home.

As with many communities of color, managing the relationship between police and the community is a massive undertaking. Nevertheless, following the protest, Alianza Dominicana was instrumental in galvanizing community leaders, youth, politicians, and the local police to discuss initiatives that would improve the relationship between young people and officers from local 34th and 33rd Precincts.

Alianza's holistic approach to service made it easier for entire families to become engaged in their programs. My mother became involved in community activism through an initiative called Mothers Against Violence, a group created to promote awareness and supportive services for women who lost their children to violence. She became aware of the plight many mothers faced in communities of color, opening her eyes to the blessing that all her children were part of the organization that kept them safe while helping their development. It also gave her insight into my activism work in the agency and community.

I spent my adolescent years in the organization, which became my first summer job, giving me the first whiff of being financially independent. I dreamed of being independent, even as a little girl. I liked the tasted of independence because I wanted to break free from the tension of my home. I did not have to depend on anyone to care for my needs. The teenager dreams of being 18 years old, but no one tells you that freedom is overrated, and adulthood lasts forever.

I emerged as a youth leader within the organization, landing me year-round part-time employment, ultimately leading to a full-time job as a Youth Organizer. It was mind-boggling to be so young and have so much autonomy. As a Youth Organizer, I created youth development initiatives that shaped or enhanced youth's leadership skills through workshops, peer education and training, community, and political activism, etc.

That political activism led me to volunteer in political campaigns that helped shape the political landscape for Dominicans in the City. I volunteered in the campaign of the first Dominican into the New York City Council, and many other first political seats for Dominicans. I also volunteered

41

for late Mayor David Dinkins campaign, who became the first African American Mayor to New York City. In 2008, I canvassed across many states for former President Barack Obama.

As a Youth Organizer, I coordinated the Youth Conference, where hundreds to thousands of young people across New York City attended La Plaza Beacon School for a day. The conference galvanized stakeholders, community leaders, politicians, and artists who provided workshops and panel discussions on issues affecting youth. The Youth Conference also offered academic scholarships, entrepreneurial, and networking opportunities for those in attendance. The excitement this event generated can only be quantified as what artists must feel when they hear thousands of people singing their songs.

The work we were doing with the youth catapulted Alianza as a leader in Youth Development field, and we were often invited to discuss best practices such as peer education and youth leadership development models at the local and national level. I had the pleasure of meeting Queen Noor of Jordan, who visited Alianza's Youth Core Group to discuss youth programming and best practices.

My role in youth development was fulfilling and ever evolving. Affording me initiatives that allowed me to supervise programs of people who, at most, were a year or a few years younger than me. Creating and implementing programs that provided support, hope, and a place where young people can be themselves is ineffable. More importantly, the opportunity to have influenced the next wave of youth leaders the way it did for me - was an honor. Being surrounded by incredible and progressive minds, and to be part of an organization that was shaping the future of thousands of families, and the community at large felt awe-inspiring.

Shit, I'm Scared

It was my last year of High School, and the only thing occupying my mind was how I would tell my mother and stepfather that I was with child.

How on earth I managed to get pregnant while being part of a Teen Pregnancy Prevention group still makes me tickle at the irony and dark humor that has been my life. Happy chaos!

I was terrified, and as luck would have it, my mother would find the pregnancy health visits card before I could tell her.

- "¿Esto es lo que te tenía enferma? ¡Eh!"
I did not respond. I slowly moved to the farthest corner of the room in case my mom threw something. I could see the disappointment on her face. As if all the dreams she thought I could accomplish vanished through the window of this pregnancy.

- "Cuando el otro (stepfather) se entere, no te atrevas a contestar."

The following mornings were a daily adventure, a treasure hunt, if I may. As I made my bed, I would find coconuts, whole eggs, and herbs under my bed. I did not know what to think of these findings. Were these protection rituals or abortion ones? That scared me even more.

Soon enough, the entire building knew I was pregnant, and my neighbors would tell me how impacted my mother was by my pregnancy. The way she told them was as if I had committed the greatest crime on earth. She failed to realize that I was scared to my core.

I worked and attended school my entire pregnancy, but at night, I would cry myself to sleep, pondering on the future. I knew I was doing the right thing by having the baby; however, the thought that I would not be a good mother terrified me.

I knew that life as I knew it would change, and I promised myself that I would use the gestation period as preparation (emotionally, financially, etc.) to afford my child a good and stable life. The thought of becoming a "statistic" unnerved me; I did not want to be one of those teen mothers who abandoned their dreams because of a child. I understood the responsibility of motherhood, and I was determined to be a good one.

Despite the fear, I was resolute in having my baby. When I was thirteen years old, a dream revealed to me that I would have a baby girl at eighteen. I spoke to her father, and he was unsure whether that was the path to go through. I left my mother's house to live with an aunt for a couple of weeks, and shortly after moved in with my daughter's father for the rest of the pregnancy. His mother cared for me, ensured I was well nourished, and controlled my anxiety.

I graduated High School that year and enrolled in college immediately. I would have my daughter during midterms, which meant returning to school shortly after giving birth.

The day I had my daughter was the first time I felt truly loved by God, and that I was holding a miracle (the second was holding my son) in my hands; it was like having a body of stars within reach. God's compensation for my troublesome beginnings. She was just hope wrapped in a blanket. When I counted her toes and fingers, saw her rosy skin against her ebony shiny hair, and those eyes that were two full moons, I was just grateful.

The relationship between my daughter's father and I utterly deteriorated, and I left him twelve days after giving birth. I never looked back. I did not have time for indecision; the energy I had left was for propelling forward, and he still was not prepared for it. I had too many goals to accomplish, the first was to provide stability for my child. Thankfully, my daughter has a beautiful relationship with her father and her paternal family.

44

I moved back home with my mother. My mom fell in love with the baby, and thought my daughter was her personal Barbie. The entire family fell in love with my daughter as she was the first everything in the house. My daughter's presence brought a softer side to everyone in the home. She brought joy, laughter, and a newness to the house that felt refreshing. Everyone in the house, especially my mother, supported me in raising my daughter so that I could pursue my academic and career goals. This time, there were no coconuts or weird herbs under the bed.

Having my daughter at a young age was a gift, and yet, that same youth was one of my most significant challenges as nothing ever prepares you for motherhood; the fears, the anxiety, and the constant questioning of whether you are doing things right. On top of that, being a single parent was challenging, but I had youth on my side. That youth was a double-edged sword because I had the energy to work, educate myself, and be present in her life, I was however, inexperienced at it.

For the first time, I began to see my mother as a person, a woman, and a mother. I understood why she was so overprotective of her children. I moved out of my mother's home a couple of months later and rented a room at a friend's house; at the time, it was all I could afford, but I wanted a space that was ours until I could afford an apartment. More importantly, I wanted to create a life that was ours, where I could instill the values that were important for my self-development while inventing a new way of parenting for my daughter (don't ask her to rate me).

Dating With Children

A few months later, I began dating Valentino, a former high school friend. Valentino was a tall, handsome, calm, and hard-working young man. We became committed quickly, partly because we had known each other for some time in High School. Valentino adored my child. There was not anything he wasn't willing to do for her.

The relationship was fun and light initially, but Valentino loved me with thorny possessiveness, and a year into the relationship, he became abusive. The first time hit me, I pressed charges against him.

As I was filing the report, the Detective following up on the case, suggested I go to the hospital in fear I might have suffered a concussion after noticing the bumps and bruises on my head and neck. That same Detective would later ask me if I was willing to drop the charges because this was his "first arrest," and he was a good guy- which was true. He was a good guy, with terrible references of what a man should be like, and no notion of self-control.

I was going to drop the charges anyway because his mother had already reached out asking for the same- except that in her eyes, I deserved the beating. You know, "esas son cosas que pasan en todas las relaciones."

Some time passed, and I went back with him. He would beat me two more times after that. I know I should have left the first time it happened or the second time, but I did not.
When you grow up being physically abused by everyone around you, as an adult, you think it's part of the process. For every beating I received as a child, someone would later "apologize" and make me believe they hit me because "they loved me." You learn to associate love with tyranny, abuse, controlling behavior, possessiveness, and jealousy.

The third time he beat me was over laundry, there were people in the house, and not one soul intervened.

I evaluated my life with him and saw the misery I would continue to endure if I stayed with him. I felt restricted as a person in that relationship. He had learned many of the misogynistic values many men adopt through their upbringing. He was dominating but not protective. Valentino expected me to wait at home for him while he spent his only day off with his friends; the time he dedicated to me revolved mostly around activities and outings with my daughter.

He loved me in the way he knew how or learned to love. I grew up in an environment where everyone could hit me, and I did not want to experience any more abuse in my life (not knowing what would come next.) It was essential to me not to expose my daughter to an environment where she was witnessing her mother being abused. Thankfully, she wasn't around for the last two beatings, and too young when the first happened.

47

A Letter to My Rapist
(Shit Keeps Happening)

I knew him from the community, Audubon Bar and Grill, other local bars, and street corners. I don't even understand how I ended up with him; there was nothing about him I was attracted to. We exchanged numbers, and as I got to know him, I found him intelligent, funny, somewhat cultured, and engaging in a bad-boy way. *There's nothing more alluring to a wounded girl than a man who smells like all the chaos and horror she's survived.*

I didn't see him as chaos because he was calm (another one.) *Some storms come with no thunder, lightning, or raucous.* He calmed me. He was that guy all your friends love, and if he's "friend-certified," you let your guard down and enjoy the ride.

The relationship blossomed organically. We spent much time together in all the perfect ways; we read poetry, discussed dreams, had good sex, laughed, and laughed. We made sense together until, one day, I found a receipt that changed everything.

It was a cold day in January, and I knew it not because the cold wind penetrated my bones but because I saw everyone holding on to their layers of clothes and coats until they arrived at safety.

I was angry. How could I not have seen this coming? I remembered him. I felt him touching, caressing, holding, and kissing me. I knew he was evil- I saw it many times, his responses, his gaze, it was in his eyes the entire time.

I walked somberly through the same streets we had walked holding hands, planning the future, and thinking, how does it happen? How does someone claim to love you yet rob you of your existence? How does a second of darkness override all shared?

It was so cold outside, but my body did not feel it; it had not felt anything for some time. I was numb. I did not feel the cold, heat, touches, or anything. For all that matter, I could have been pronounced dead. Some say that to be pronounced dead, your heart must stop working; the problem was my heart was no longer working; it hadn't since that day, but it was beating, and I was breathing, so to pronounce me dead was medically impossible, as oxygen was flowing through my nostril and into my lungs.

I was breathing (barely), not enough, but enough to make it from one day to the next. I had no "soul". I was a walking zombie, still besotted by him. How do you love your rapist? How do you remain faithful to emotion after the most heinous of betrayals? I had so many questions but no answers.

As I walked the streets, I felt him beating me, beating my soul out of existence, pushing it to the farthest dimensions of the universe until eternity itself - rejected me. I should have listened. I heard myself saying, "Just sleep and don't wake up." Do not wake up, get dressed, shower, or move. I did not listen to my intuition. I did not want to go to that party. It was a celebration of life. It was supposed to be. It ended in the celebration of life for one and the end of another.   They say that for every newborn, another person must die. I did not physically die, but my soul died as it left my body.

I died on January 10, 2000. Ten days into a new millennium, and this was my beginning.

Rape is the physical violation of the body, an emotional tearing of the soul, and the ripping of your heart into pieces. It takes every breath from your existence but leaves you enough air to breathe.

This story is about redemption, about finding peace amid chaos. It is about looking at the Devil straight into his eyes and declaring, "I Am stronger." If you are not a rape survivor, know that as you read this chapter, three other women are getting raped or sexually assaulted by their lover, spouse, uncle, dad, and or friend before you end the next few pages.

Responsible for my rape was my insatiable pursuit of love. Love, consistently placing me at the center of highly noxious situations for a taste of it.

The Lie

Why was he there? I don't know, I pitied him. Limerence. When you are young, you let the idea of love rule, think, and make decisions for you. You feel the current love affair is one of the greatest stories ever, and you're the protagonist. That is why he was there because everyone wants to be part of a love story that changes lives, that gives little girls in bed the hope that one day, they too, can have such a story.

He was there because *Pity and Love* become the same at one point. Because there is this long-awaited moment where one feels pitying, pardoning, and forgiving is redemptive. Forgiveness equates to love, and one is good at heart for being able to do so. Therefore, you turn the other cheek only to get slapped in the name of "salvation."

I learned that he and his "ex-girlfriend" were expecting a baby. She was six months pregnant; we had been together for a year when I found out. He claimed it was a moment in which he could not say no. He asserted that he did not know that she was pregnant. She didn't tell him (what a bitch! I thought). It is unfair for any woman to exclude a man from his paternal right. Knowing that she denied him for so many months, I could not leave him; I mean, how could I leave him? It is not that he was avoiding responsibility. No, he was denied, the way criminals are denied their rights. Poor man, I thought, so no, I didn't leave him.

I was determined to help him. We discussed the pregnancy, and I got involved as if it were our baby. I went as far as picking out names for his unborn child. Right now, a child is walking the earth, my rapist's child, and I named the child!

The truth must reveal itself - as above, so below, and everything under the sun is exposed. His mother told me it was a lie, and he knew all along. She also had forewarned me about him not being a "good person," to which I thought,

51

"No wonder he's broken; what mother speaks like that about her son?" *There's no bigger sin than the person who refuses to hear when the river is clamoring.*

He knew she was pregnant, so much so that he sent her to live in another state (bastard!). Far enough that I wouldn't find out and close enough to his relatives so they could look after her and the baby, it dawned on me his urgency to move to Georgia! Yes, Atlanta would have been far away enough that I would have never suspected his infidelity.

Thinking of him possibly leaving for Atlanta for good saddened me, leading me to adopt Gladys Knight's *"Midnight Train"* as my anthem. Oh, how it saddened me every time I heard the song, the thought that he would leave for Georgia and leave me behind.

I felt so blindsided by the revelation. How gullible was I? How did I not see it? The clues were there. The clues were always there, and I refused to acknowledge them. I was afraid to put the pieces together; "knowing" forces introspection, which will open Pandora's box, and once opened - a decision must be made, forcing you to close the box.

Months prior, I found money transfer receipts in his drawer which he sent to his ex, not in large quantities, but sent frequently. I questioned him about the transfers; of course, I asked. His excuse was that he sent his ex-girlfriend money because of pity, for his ex was going through a tough time financially. Her mother practically abandoned her to her luck, that she had done so much for him, he was grateful (and, I thought, what caliber of a man, what a man, wow, a decent, grateful, protective, lovely man, and he's, my man.)

A part of me felt so proud to have such a nobleman by my side, and I believed him and left it at that. How could I judge him? I know what it is like to feel gratitude. I did so many things in my life out of gratitude. I stayed with people out of gratitude, in relationships that were not working out because of gratitude. I pretended it was something else—

something like love, but when I rested my head on the pillow, I knew it was gratitude. I kept friendships, and they kept me around out of gratitude. Gratitude keeps people in abusive relationships. Some people will never materialize their destiny because of gratitude to their parents, society, or unknown factors. Gratitude is a virtue, nonetheless. What a virtuous man, I thought. I understood the meaning and sacrifice behind the word "gratitude" and wanted to be part of it, too.

But time passed, and the pieces to the puzzle started to piece themselves.

Destiny must fulfill itself, and I could not be with him after knowing he blatantly lied to me all those months. His touch disgusted me. I felt him touching her as he made love to me. I felt her saliva, telling me that "he was still her man; I'm just an intruder." He had the opportunity to tell me. He knew I hated lies. He lied about her, he lied about not knowing, and he lied about loving her. I chose to leave him.

One November morning, he called to update me about his life. He told me that he did not go back to her. He did not love her. He wanted to be there for her, for the baby, but not romantically. He did not love her. He was about to lose his place.

Something about the fall makes me more vulnerable than at other times of the year because I relate to the fall in my own life. The way foliage changes colors and leaves fall to the ground, exposing trees to their nakedness in preparation for winter. The death of all brings about the much-needed respite and rebirth for Spring.

I felt terrible for him. I pitied him. I felt so bad for him but did not want to help him. I was hurt. He lied, I reminded myself, but people like me do not allow others to suffer (The Savior Complex). I now understand that it wasn't my good nature after all, but a trauma response, where I break my boundaries to alleviate the suffering of others.

After he hung up, I sat on my couch, the same couch that embraced me as I sank into disillusion when I learned the pregnancy news.

I contemplated if this was another lie, a manipulative tactic to loop me back in. I sat on my couch, excogitating his future and the right thing to do. I asked God for guidance, and God responded, "NO." I pretended that I didn't hear God's "No." I'm human, weak, and afraid to listen to my inner voice because it has disappointed me so many times. I did not listen to God and justified it by telling myself I was doing a good deed, and as the adage goes, "The road to hell is paved with good intention," it will surely slap me right into hades.

He moved into my place, I gave him rules and boundaries, and he became my roommate. I went to work and came back; he "dique" looked for work.

I am still in limerence of him.

Time cures all evils; I did not believe I could ever have a good rapport with him after he lied.

One night of drinking, having a good time, and discussing life matters, the world seemed as it was before the ex, the pregnancy, and the lies.

The liquor robbed me of all my senses (this is an excuse to justify what I wanted to do,) of my dignity, and I forgot I was mad at him.

There was only bread and Tropicana orange juice in the refrigerator, but to us, it felt as if we were at Cipriani's eating a four-course-meal with the most expensive champagne.

As the liquor dominated the night, I wanted to relieve our romance. He touched me, and I thought I missed it; I did miss it. He entered my home once again.   At that moment, he was mine, and I was his. It was an incomparable amount of pleasure mixed with what I thought was love.

There was a blackout in the city that night, which rendered itself to a perfect night of lovemaking on a New York City fire escape. It was perfect! And a mistake by sunrise.

He thought things changed, but they had not. I was hurt, and a perfect night was not enough to make me forget that he had lied. I told him it was a night. It won't happen again; you are still a tenant in this house. You are not my boyfriend. He wanted to die. He said he would. I said, okay!

The first month passed, and he had not found work or a place to stay. I needed him out of my house. He was still looking at me the same way. He was still looking at me as his girlfriend. I wasn't, and it was getting too complicated for me emotionally.

He needed to leave. I spoke to him and gave him another month. I wasn't his girlfriend. I wanted to be, but I wasn't therefore, I shouldn't care what happened, but I did. I understood that pain does not rid you of your human qualities, morals, or social responsibilities to others.   I care for people for their well-being. I care for 'humanity' and always have; just because he hurt me did not mean I shouldn't worry about his agony. I wanted to find a middle ground where I could detach from him yet still be helpful. I couldn't because as much as I tried to deny it, I still had feelings for him. I still wondered how it would be if he hadn't lied. I felt trapped in a wheel where the outcome was always the same. I was still in pain, so when I helped, I felt naive, and when I detached, I felt horrendous, and far removed from God.

Rape is defined as forced sexual intercourse, including psychological and physical coercion. What the definition lacks is that it is Coercion of the Soul.

Yes, Coercion of the Soul. The soul is compromised to become something that, in its natural state, had the infraction not happened, would have never been altered, thus, remaining intact and healthy.

At that point, one's soul becomes non-existent. A disconnect between the body and the soul happens instantaneously as the rape occurs. I believe it happens before, as the conscious mind recognizes the threat of being assaulted. The soul leaves and disconnects from the body. I know. I saw my soul leaving my body.

I was non-existent. I was barely walking. The physical pain I could endure. I could not tolerate the violation of my being, my wholeness. Little by little, I was stripped of my dignity, and the fabric of my life decomposed in nine miserable hours. Compared to a lifetime, nine hours may seem minute. Those nine hours were enough to destroy countries- it was enough to ruin my life.

He did this. He tore the fabric of my being, my dignity, in nine hours. But what happens to an individual to drive them to perform such heinous crimes against a loved one? He claimed to love me. I thought he loved me. How could he? He was a thief. He took all the love and support I had offered him and took my soul without my consent. Rapists should be punished for taking of the soul without consent.

My body has the resiliency to heal itself- the bruises, the pain, the body heals itself rapidly. The soul? - Different story. It would take years, what felt like an eternity to assemble it back together.

The Party

We arrived home from the party around 2:30 a.m., I did not want him to come to my house. My intuition told me I was in danger, and he would take my soul with him. It would be one of the most significant challenges I faced (forgiving myself for putting myself in that situation).

He barged into my bedroom- the same one that had welcomed him many times. The same bedroom that was a witness to all the lovemaking between us. He proceeded to slap me, questioning why I was playing games with him. I answered that I was not playing games and did not want to be with him anymore.

"You lied", he said.
I responded, "You haven't?"
"Not to you."
"Yes, you have."
He slapped me again, and suddenly, I understood the danger that awaited me. As my cheeks received the impact of his fingers on my face, my eyes opened wide, and my heart started beating fast. I was in the red zone. I took a good look at him. His eyes were bulging red. He was furious, and his voice turned deep, scary deep. He grabbed, and slapped me once again, and said, "This will teach you to respect me."

How had I disrespected him? I thought, isn't it the other way around? This is some crazy shit! I get cheated on, I get lied to, and I am the disrespectful one?
I snapped out and slapped him back. He was in disbelief that I hit him back. He punched me, and I felt it in my bones. He grabbed me by the hair and dragged me to the closet, slamming my body into it. I felt my tendons and muscle tissue tearing apart as the tip of a metal nail pinched my back as my body hit the closet door.

The body is so resilient that it would find ways to resist within the first hour. It gets used to it; how we get used to having someone around and calling it love. The psychological and emotional abuse was what was tiring my body.

As he began tearing apart my nightgown, my mind started wandering. In my daze, I remembered a night after coming home from a nightclub, awakened by his voice. I couldn't quite understand what he was saying initially; his voice was meager and groggy as if speaking under his teeth. What I thought I did hear was him saying:
"The prostitute was getting raped. That they were going to rape her. He said that she was in danger, someone help her." I didn't understand then, and I kept asking him, "Who was getting raped? Who was raping the prostitute?"
He was sleep talking. He never said who she was or who did it and sank back into sleep. I told him about it the following day, and he told me "He must have been dreaming- he didn't know." My mind began to question if this is what he does. Did he rape the prostitute the way he was raping me? Was he the rapist?

The cold, pointy metal brought me back to reality, pinching my throat. I assumed he had already stabbed me; he hadn't. He passed the knife through my hair and pointed it at my scalp and the back of my neck. I'm impatient by nature. The fact that patience was the big lifesaver terrified me more than the situation itself, but I did it, funny ha! How we adapt to things in fear of death. No es lo mismo llamar el Diablo, que verlo llegar.
I sucked up all my fear and waited. Wait. Wait to see if exhaustion would have him stop or wait until he killed me. I asked him, how do you love? Is this your ultimate way of showing it? How do you do this to me? I reminded him of who I was. I tried reminding him that he "loved me." I have been nothing but good in his life; Why repay me this way? I began questioning why he was raping me; what pleasure could he get out of forcing me into this when he had me so

many times? But in this case, the rape was about him mind-fucking me. It was to leave me scarred.

He knew that he had no attachments to me. His assaulting me was deep enough that I would spend my entire lifetime dealing with this as you deal with a child.

He knew I would not have children with him; the trauma was the child he left me. Men tend to think that you are unavailable or undesirable because you have children. It's as if your house were damaged, therefore depreciating in value. He left me with a torn vagina, heart, and a soulless body instead of a child.

The violation was merely a way for him to regurgitate the trauma I worked so hard to leave behind. But he was clever, more than I thought. He knew that he was making me relive my childhood. He knew it would send me into a steep darkness. That there were not enough lifetimes to make me recuperate from this. He was stamping my future in an abyss with my thoughts forever in the gutter.

I would be scared to be touched or loved by another man. Even if I tried - his face and that of my childhood molester would haunt me. Now is a double knock-out. This is harder to put behind.

I asked him to think of his child! As those words finished coming out of my mouth, he realized what he was doing was terrible. His expression changed from enraged to surprised (as if he had disassociated himself for a moment and realized what he had done).

Everything changed again; he turned me around, and I felt the pressure as he penetrated my anus. He insisted that I find pleasure in it. He insisted that he wanted to satisfy me. He insisted that it felt good as he destroyed my rectum. I told him this was not pleasurable, and his behavior was not normal. That smell still haunts me today: the smell of sabotage, destruction, desperation, and inability to tolerate the pain or the torment that his sodomizing did to me.

I think about it today, and it still sends chills down my spine.

Desperate situations call for desperate measures. Sometimes, in my line of work, I would hear stories and say, God, how or why would you put up with this? Wasn't there a way for you to have dealt with it better? The reply was often as simple as "Sometimes, when you are desperate, you must do the unthinkable to survive." I tried reasoning with him, appealing to his humanity. I asked him to leave, that I would not say anything, that I would not call the cops, but to leave me alone. The thought that I could even think of calling anyone on him seethed him further.

He retook me, this time penetrating while choking me. I tried to defend myself as much as possible, throwing punches as hard as possible, as often as possible. I was not going to be subdued by this monster. I was not going to allow fear to make me a victim. If I was going to die, I was going to give him a fight for it. I would not give him the satisfaction of taking me out so easily.
Five hours had gone by of this torture—five hours of cruelty. By then, he had put a knife to my throat as I refused to sleep with him willingly. He had choked me and repeatedly beaten me. I wonder how much longer this was going to last. He said, "I would be with him whether I wanted it or not." He had taken me as many times as he wanted. He said, "I was to do what he asked me to do." I refused; I was scared and confused, and this could not be him.

Everyone has a human side, I thought! Unfortunately, there is no human side in moments of darkness. He was not human at that time. I got tired of reasoning, and I was getting mad. I kept saying to myself, an Angel must come down. God's children are always protected. Something will happen. Lord, make it soon. Please. I began talking to him about God. In one of the tussles, I attempted to kneel and started praying.

If mentioning his daughter upset him, talking about God was worse. Oh, he became enraged with my kneeling to pray. He ordered me to get back up. Twice, I said no, the third and fourth, I was too afraid. I felt like Peter when he denied Jesus. I felt like Judas Iscariot. I was terrified, tired, and powerless.

I saw the devil with my own eyes. There's a saying in my country, "It is not the same calling the Devil as seeing him with your own eyes." I saw him that day. I had always wondered what he looked like, and that day, I found out. I slept with him for so long and welcomed him by opening the doors to my heart and house. I sheltered him. I comforted him in times of pain. I fed him. I gave him my love in and out. I fed every one of his desires. My visions of him were nothing like reality. He was unlike any paintings I had ever seen, there were no horns or demonic-looking wings.

It was the eyes.

The eyes had more intensity than a volcano. They were vivid red, big, bulging red eyes. I dropped the bible and got up the way he ordered me. "Lord, this man is going to kill me. Lord do not forsake me." As I got up, he asked me, where is your God? I'm unsure if fear or the fact that he was mocking God, but I looked him straight in his eyes and, with a cracked voice, told him, "You're looking at him."

Up until that point, I had done whatever I could not to make him think I was afraid. I was dying of fear; no human being could tell me I did not understand fear. I breathed it all my life. I feared success, failure, and love, but no fear amounts to this kind of fear. It was terrorizing. It was dehumanizing. It's an unutterable kind of fear. It was a dark and forceful energy. I have never known this kind of fear.

After this experience, I can overcome anything. But I am a survivor, and I am a fighter. I fought for my life and punched whenever I could, but I was also physically exhausted by this point.

Exhaustion was not an answer and would not let me out alive. I thought to outsmart and fight harder, but the devil is resilient. I was running out of options.

I punched him with all the strength and pain in my body right into his testicles.

I grabbed them until one began bleeding. I told him repeatedly, "I am stronger than him, than this or whatever he could do to me. I am stronger, mentally, and emotionally."

I told him I pitied him, that he was just giving me more reasons to detest him. God allowed this to happen so I could see how much love he lacked.

Moreover, I would see him pay ten-folds for what he was doing to me. I would love again (I knew that after what he did to me, I would never love again.) But I could not let him walk away thinking that if I survived this, he would have tainted me to the point that I could never be receptive to love again.

I knew I was lying. I needed to appear firmer because it was the only way to tackle a bully, even as he took my body repeatedly without permission or consent. Even if he tore my vagina beyond repair..., psychologically, or spiritually - I did not let him win. He was a loser in my eyes. I had control. I told him that my strength transcended his wickedness.

He stopped out of exhaustion and went to his room to nap (yes, he slept). I wanted to go in there and kill him, but I had no strength left.

I cried and bathed until the fire hydrants in New York City were depleted of water. I washed my body until I was three shades lighter. I called my friends, and they called my sister. They all came to my aid.

I went to work the next day.

I was stronger.

I did not report him. I know that by not reporting him,
I contributed to the list of rapists freely walking the earth.
I knew that I could be jeopardizing someone else. I became another statistic. But I was too embarrassed, too ashamed.

I protected him, his family, and my dignity - whatever was left. Who would believe that a woman with a child gets raped by her ex-boyfriend, who boards a room in her house?

Truthfully, I was protecting my abuser more than myself. The way we protect the family members while subjecting the victim to commingling with their abuser at holiday parties. The way victims walk by the altars of the dead who abused us, altars set by our loved ones, despite knowing that the deceased is not worthy of an altar.

The way we protect "Los trapitos del sol" while eviscerating the sanctity of our soul, our minds, and our healing. Women are taught to protect everyone else but themselves. To forgive fully is the Christian thing to do, right? I knew no one would have believed it; therefore, I kept quiet, like so many other women.

I could not believe that this took place in my own home. I was held hostage in my own house by my ex-boyfriend, who lied, cheated on me, impregnated someone else, and, to add insult to injury, raped and beat me.

Those nine hours felt like nothing in comparison to the following months. I relived that night at least a thousand times after that. He threatened to kill me or anyone he thought I shared the information with. He would show up to my daughter's school and my job to remind me that if I spoke, I knew what would come and that I should know what he was capable of by now. I felt hostage in my skin. The bruises, the pain in my back, and my torn vagina will never compare to what happened to my soul.
The psychological turmoil was as traumatizing as the event itself.

My life continued as per usual. As if those hours had not occurred, but this is how I was raised- move past it. It already happened. Don't talk about it. Don't think about it. Sweep it under the rug. I went to work every day and continued with my academic journey. I met with my friends for drinks as if nothing ever happened. During the daytime, I was busy and preoccupied with life's matters, but at nightfall, it terrified me as it did when I was a little girl. The fear that he would break into my apartment haunted me.

I kept putting one foot in front of the other. I kept praying to God to heal my heart and thoughts. I kept reminding myself that I had power and overcame many trials before this one. I got into therapy once again. I read self-help and development books to soothe my soul. I cried when no one watched. And sometimes, the tears would just bathe me in public.

I don't remember when it happened, but I began feeling as if my soul allowed some sunlight to penetrate my body. Little by little, I began to feel the effects of the cold and the heat. The hours in my days began regulating themselves. Hope hugged me again. My soul recharged. My vagina began its healing process.

God's children are always protected.

I was stronger.

A Letter to My Rapist

Dear rapist,

It has been five years and a few weeks since that horrible night when you aspired to strip me of my dignity, future, sanity, and sense of self-worth.

I guess that as your 36th birthday is approaching, you're going through a period of self-discovery and emotional balance in your chaotic life. Nonetheless, whatever is causing this desire to change your ways indicates that you possess a certain level of consciousness, making you human.

After processing what you said today, I am still determining if you are contrite. I think you are using the excuse that "you do not recollect that night" to not deal with your guilt. I mean, how can you forget? I guess that "not remembering" makes you feel less guilty. People apologize for things they're genuinely sorry for to end, bring closure, and move on.

How unfair that is to the person who was wronged. I mean, to forgive an offense that the perpetrator feels no remorse for and does not understand the devastating effects their actions caused is as cruel as the offense itself.

Why would you commit such a heinous crime against someone who did absolutely nothing but be good to you?

As I digress into that night, I recall being in bed the entire time, not wanting to cook the dish I would take to the party. I remember feeling crippling anxiety. Finally, I got up and just went to the party. I remember being by the stairs and you bugging out. Had I known what was awaiting me at the house, I would have never let you intimidate me into going to the house.

I think of that night, and it all seems like a dramatic movie. For nine hours, for nine fucking hours, you beat me repeatedly, raped me repeatedly, held a knife to my throat, tore up my nightgown (Is it coming back to you now, are you starting to recollect?).

As I told you that night, "I'm stronger than you. There are two moments that, until this day, have boggled my mind. One was "my asking you to stop in your daughter's name and you telling me not to bring her into this. The other was when I knelt to pray, thinking that I would not come out of it alive, and your tone changed into a more profound and groggier tone, ordering me to get up, put the bible down, and stop praying with your bulging red eyes.
I started fighting back at some point, taking every punch but punched and slapped right back. Exhaustion made you stop. You had the audacity even to take a nap in my house. The home I had opened to you so you could get your life together.

If you got to this page, then the only thing I can ask you is, to be honest with yourself. If this is a genuine attempt to rectify all that you have done, then do what you know is suitable for all you have done, not just to me but to innocent people who did not deserve your actions.

I tell you that having a good, clean heart is good; it's the only thing that will provide you with serenity.

Life has not been the same for me; it will never be the same. But thank you because you only caused me to reevaluate my worth. Albeit I've dealt with many more of life's trials after that, here I am, as strong as I can be, impacting the lives of others and helping others through my despair or devastation.

I'm wrong, and you did not destroy me. You disrupted my life a bit and made me see that love exists and is real. You have not, and no one else will ever take the right from me to live and love openly and give my all to someone receptive to it.

Thanks to you, I do not have to sell myself short by having a mediocre, sharing kind of love. I have yet to find that person, but he will come. I just know it. I deserve it. But in the meantime, I will continue experiencing love in different ways through my family, children, friends, people I serve, and God!

I pray your daughter never experiences what you did to me. No woman should ever experience that.

As for you, I forgave you a long time ago. I hope you forgive yourself for how you've led your life (so much talent wasted on malicious acts).
Life is what you make of it. I choose to live differently. I will continue to pray for you and your loved ones. May God give you peace, wisdom, and character to overcome temptation and follow your chosen path!

I'm okay. I am stronger.

Sincerely,

Laying In a Cactus Bed

Thinking of love
Thoughts of hatred came to mind,
All the baggage, the hurt, the pain,
The years of strain
when I gave up the world for a simple kiss
and got kicked in the ribs.
These are the thoughts that flow through my mind when I
think of love.

Thinking of roses, ha, what do I think?
Their smell makes me sick.
Thoughts of tumultuous times come to mind,
When rose petals stung me like a bee,
Where the only thing growing in my garden
were cactuses, and that's
where I laid my head to sleep.

The color purple became part of me,
as my bruises sunk into my skin
And that's what came to mind when I think of roses…

Am I bitter, sour or sweet?

My Sun Is Born

The rapist did not leave me alone. For months, he taunted and harassed me, and I thought I was losing my mind with the pressure I was under. In comes Bebe!

Bebe, a guy I knew from the neighborhood, appeared out of nowhere in my life. Every day, he waited for me on the corner of his block with an R&B CD, a rose and walked me home. Unbeknownst to him, he was protecting me through this gesture. To get home, I had to pass by the rapist's block. I had changed routes many times, but he would catch me.

One day, as Bebe and I were walking, the rapist walked towards us. In an impulse, I grabbed Bebe's hand and clawed my nails into him. Bebe caught the interaction immediately and proceeded to interlace his fingers with mine. When we got to my building, he asked what happened between me and that guy. My intuition told me to tell him what happened.

The following day, Bebe waited for me as he always did, with a CD and, this time, a bouquet of red roses (my favorites). I don't know how he knew those were my favorites, but he did. He greeted me by the nickname he gave me- Sunshine Smile, kissed me on the cheek, and told me that "the rapist would never bother me again. That he spoke to him man to man, and he would never harm me again." I am unsure what Bebe told him, but the rapist left me alone, at least with the audacity to approach me.

I felt so protected by Bebe. I knew he had feelings for me, but we were just friends. He did not need to do that. I felt immense gratitude towards him. Several weeks passed when he asked me out, and I said yes.

Bebe and I had three things in common: a love of music, comedy, and our skin color. Bebe was kind, funny, hard-working, flashy, and delusional. He should have pursued a career in writing because his stories were straight out from a

70

Sci-fi movie. He had a way with words and the gift of persuasion. Fast forward some time, and I was pregnant. I have never seen anyone be so happy to hear pregnancy news, especially because Bebe already had children. It is as if the pregnancy news brought him back to life.

He proposed seven months into the pregnancy, to be precise, the day my dog died (he wasn't very good at timing). I said yes.

I took the ring to Joyeria Pepe before having it appraised. The jeweler stated, "he understood objects have sentimental value, but not to take the trip downtown." I should have been upset, but I knew Bebe too well to know that the ring was not 3.5 carats and knew he meant well. I wore my fake ring.

He ensured I always had flowers in the house and felt safe. He made the pregnancy so comfortable and joyous. My son joined us one hot day in June with Bebe and my mother by my side every step of the way.

When I saw my son for the first time, I felt love hug my body. He was born small, yet so perfect! I could hold him in one palm, as he was so tiny. His black hair and sweet almond eyes were like the sun looking at me and warming every particle of my being.

My daughter is my moon, and my son is my Sun. They have been eclipsing since birth. A constellation of joy and hope produced from my womb.

I just felt grateful that they chose me (why? I would never understand) to be their mother. Having experienced such tumultuous experiences with men, I felt the pressure of raising my son to be a man of character, honest, decent, loving, kind, and happy. *Happy, principled men don't damage people.* I wanted that for my son.

The relationship with Bebe began deteriorating rapidly after our son was born. Tension began building during the pregnancy, although not completely of his doing, but his lack of boundaries with his former partners intensified the tension at home. I was already helping to raise his eldest son, and the constant pressures in the home made me feel that I was left to my own to deal with all the emotional, and financial instability that was taking place.

Women check out emotionally, men check out physically. I was done! I was tired. I was tired of my responsibilities and carrying his. Tired of "time" and its games, of always showing up late to everything. I checked out. I tempted fate, I played with it. I was defying her, defying my expectations, my own limited restrictions. I met a man whom I wanted to risk it all for... And would eventually go for it!

While I wanted the relationship with Bebe to work out for the sake of my son and daughter, for the sake of stability, but in my heart, I knew I was not in love with him. I loved and cared for him, but it was a love based on gratitude. I felt protected, but our differences were too significant to bridge with appreciation. I stayed as long as I could. I was grateful that he gave my son. But that was not going to change the fact that my heart did not belong to him.

Remembering Love:
"The Science Project"

I don't watch novelas because I grew tired of the same plot delivered by different faces. The typical Spanish soap opera goes something like this: Girl meets boy (usually affluent), they kiss, they fall in love, and have a baby. The baby gets stolen and raised by some evil bitch (antagonist) that wants the male protagonist. They separate because the antagonist fakes a pregnancy. The good girl chooses to leave the protagonist as she feels betrayed and as an intruder.

Usually, the leading male suffers an accident, resulting in memory loss. After a ridiculous, okay, let's call it a miraculous event, he regains memory; only to discover the truth (usually 5 to ten years later)! After this discovery, he goes on an endless quest to find the poor, defenseless protagonist, who is as wealthy as he is. They finally reunite to live happily ever after.

Until I met the Science Project, I thought these stories were conjured up by people with great imaginations due to being lonely children (like me). It is not the case; these stories are as accurate as the ones I lived, and many people live them. That is why I felt compelled to tell you this story.

This chapter is about a story of love. A love story, or so I thought.

73

I have always considered myself strong-minded, willful, and with clear aspirations. As a matter of fact, by the age of five, I knew exactly how my life would plan out. I was to become a lawyer between the ages of 23 and 25, famous by 28, with a beautiful home and everything that makes all soap operas so attractive. However, life and its ironies had something set out for me that was different from what I had planned.

Always have a plan B, I always heard; well, the phrase is not in vain. You better have more than a plan B to be ready to deal with all the plot twists life inevitably has for each of us.

Much of my existence has centered around relationships, perchance, to validate the fragmented parts of my childhood, and thus, I invested much of myself into making relationships work. I have experienced this polarity around relationships where I wanted to be in a loving relationship but never hesitated to pick up and leave, if need be, as men were projects to me. It may sound harsh, "men as projects," but it was easier to adapt to this concept as self-preservation to protect my dignity and soul.

There was a point in my life when I thought that my sole purpose was to rehabilitate all the crackheads (they were not drug addicts but acted as such) that came into my life.

You have heard of these men. The type of man that would be unwelcomed in your mother's home. The kind of men that make you think that becoming a lesbian is always a better option than dealing with one of them again men.

Yes, I rehabilitated them. Once the rehabilitation process was complete, they would leave to live a "normal and happy" life with the next woman (as that is my lot in life.)

I began thinking that I was the problem and that my "issues" got in the way of having a loving and healthy relationship. But no, I have come to accept that no matter how open, pleasant, tolerant, and decent you are..., men will always be men; as the saying goes, "Cuando no lo hacen a la entrada, lo hacen a la salida" (They're bound to mess up eventually.)

I love, and I love deeply, but I knew that men would come and go; therefore, I never stopped doing things I loved because I was "in love." I refused to lose my individuality or stop breathing because I was involved with someone. I always understood that 'love' does not mean relinquishing your life (experience would teach me that I loved with limitations).

As a result, I have come to embrace that I may be more in love with the concept of love than love itself (blame my Venus in Aquarius). I always keep the door open for love. I give it all I have, give myself completely, under the condition that I am not lied to. I do not tolerate lies, betrayals, or cheating (this will all catch up with me; now keep reading). My motto was, "Do as you please. Don't let me find out." Some took the advice, and others took it as a challenge; this taught me that *"The idea of fidelity is as clear to men as having a penis is to women."*

I admit it: I am in love with love. I love - love. I am a love-a-holic. I am a love adventurer. I will climb mountains to find it and starve for days for a glance of love. I am always seeking true love, the perfect love, the perfect man, the ideal relationship, and situation.

- but always ending up with the exact opposite.

I met the Science Project in Science class while pursuing my Undergraduate degree. He was leaning against the wall wearing a blue cap, a t-shirt that read "I Am," light denim jeans, and black sneakers. We locked eyes for what felt like an eternity to me but were merely seconds.

He was in his thirties, with no kids (10 points for that. I have children but did not want to get involved with men who had children). I did not like the drama that comes with being in a relationship with men who have children. Hypocrite, you might call me, as I have two of my own, but if I have learned anything, men and women deal with life differently. Though I had two children of my own, I knew that before engaging in any relationship, boundaries had to be put in place. Most men aren't great at setting limits or boundaries between their former and their new partner without there being some tension. Since my life was already full of drama, I was ensuring I had manageable drama.

Back to my dream guy. He was delectable, what a body! Ahh! Before seeing him as his mother brought him into this world, I had already sculpted his body in the way the shirt hugged his big bulgy arms and his thick neck marked by light brown birthmarks. I always imagined that his neck indicated what rested below (and it was)! His legs were as defined as the rest of his body; His physique reminded me of Greek sculptures—he was my Adonis.

It was not love at first sight; I was intrigued at first sight, though. He was delicious eye candy, but I was still with Bebe. Nevertheless, it was impossible to negate the attraction between us. It was the synergy rooted in faith, peace, and curiosity - it felt spiritual. It felt as though God was participating in it, in us. This energy was empowering, enveloping, and addictive.

Perhaps the improbability of a relationship manifesting made it more addictive. Our connection was the kind that spoke to great friendships, as if we were going to be around each other for years to come. A tingling sensation took hold of me from the soles of my feet to crown of my head whenever he was next to me. I felt all my organs harmoniously communicating, producing unintentional laughter. I felt joy.

We got along very well with occasional flirting, but nothing more. He was a great conversationalist; I loved that we talked about everything and everyone. It had been a long time since I met a man I could talk to for hours on the phone and not necessarily talk about himself or trying to get into my pants. For me, that was a turn-on. The school projects forced us to spend much time together, and I soon made excuses to spend time with him on the weekends, and we became close friends. He knew I was in a relationship (unfulfilling, but I was in a relationship), and he was single. I was already working on an exit strategy from the relationship with Bebe, but I was still there, and guilt set in.

One mundane Thursday, we decided to skip class and go for drinks at the Fusion Lounge on 54th and 10th Avenue. After a few rounds of drinks, he leaned in for a kiss, and I melted into him with all the desires I had been suppressing. That kiss. That kiss was the catalyst for everything. Until that kiss, I was forcing myself to stay in my situation out of gratitude. But that kiss spoke to every cell in my body and soul, confirming that I couldn't stay with Bebe anymore.

Of course, I had a past before that kiss, but it felt like he wiped out my entire history in one kiss. My present started that Thursday night at the Fusion lounge, and my heart wanted to be with him. He set the bar for my future and how someone should kiss me if he were not around.

It was that first kiss that did it for me. I could blame it on the liquor, but that would not explain the other ten thousand kisses. I could kiss him an entire night without the need to make love, not because I didn't want to, but because kissing him was utopia. His kisses calmed all my irrational resistance, soothing all the trauma that protruded through my pores. It contained and excited me at the same time. I found myself at home in his mouth, in my comfort zone; I felt safe. His kisses became a security blanket.

He kissed the way every woman should and wants to be kissed, not in a rush, but with intention, with enough intensity and softness to make you want to take it all off in the street. The tongue becomes the rustling to the nervous system to surrender contempt and into the tenderness of a kiss. The tongue creates the perfect environment for a seductive play of pleasure and delight. It was the kind of kiss where your hair, eyes, and body are as equally important as your lips. That type of kiss attests to how much one is cared for because it is done with the utmost care and caution. His kiss transported me to the beauty of infinity and proved how cruel being mortal is.

What I felt for my Science Project was more potent than my gratitude for Bebe. After trying for three years, I ended the relationship with Bebe in May of that year. I began dating the Science Project in August. I did not need labels with him because I felt perfectly safe in whatever "we were." Each day served to solidify our friendship; the desire and need to be with one another grew stronger. Our paths inevitably became tied- it was too much of a good thing.

It was freeing to date him, to proclaim the nights with him - even if only on the phone. There were no interruptions. The nights belonged to us; there was room for nothing else, just our voices. We waited for the night like the Owls do. We spoke on the phone until my eyes tired, only to go to sleep and wake up with his voice as my alarm.

When we made love, he became another person with me. He was an animal; he was insatiable, and so was I. He became obsessed with my body, mapping my beauty marks to kiss them gently. He knew every curvature of my body. It felt as if this was not the first time, we had been together; he knew me from many lives ago, he knew what made me go crazy, and he was tender yet so animalistic! It was perfect.

Inhibitions were out the window (we were both competitive by nature), and when we got together, it was the perfect opportunity to show off tricks under the belt. Never a dull moment, every time was an Olympic event. Everything went with us, and this did not diminish the level of respect.

But all this excitement was usually interrupted by my secrets, thoughts, and whatever perturbed him.

I spent every other weekend at his house. Oh! I looked forward to those weekends. I enjoyed being with my children, but being a single parent can sometimes be overwhelming. All the responsibilities fall on you. You become your children—your outings are childlike. Those weekends with my Science Project were my adult moments. I felt free, unattached, without responsibilities other than making love and having fun with this hot guy. Honestly, for 48 hours - that felt great!

No matter what kind of day we had, we knew everything would be okay when we saw each other. We cherished our time together. We talked about our day and then put everything in the back of our minds so that we could enjoy our company.

Another quality I loved about him was his ability to stay present in the moment. It's as if he intuited losing something and, therefore, had to embrace and bask in the moment, whatever that moment was.

Rape victims or people who have endured severe trauma often experience flashbacks of the event(s). I experienced the most horrifying flashbacks in one of our earlier love-making moments. I began screaming, kicking, and asking him to get off me. He was bemused at my reaction and asked if he had done something wrong. That very question consumed me with shame and fear. I did not want him to think (or confirm) I was crazy and left me for good. He sensed my anxiety and sat me on his lap like a little girl chatting with her father. He caressed my hair and asked again, what was wrong?

His tenderness in that moment made me feel so sheltered, and I confessed to him that I had been raped a few years prior and molested as a child, and for some odd reason, I saw my uncle's face while he was on top of me. He cried and hugged me, asking why I hadn't shared that information with him earlier. He hugged me so tight that I felt our heartbeats beating synchronously. No man had ever held me so gently that I felt engulfed in pure love and empathy; that moment changed our story. It calmed all the voices in my head around safety, love, and vulnerability about what happened to me. It helped him understand why I was so guarded and defensive. It helped him become more vulnerable with me as well. What began as a casual exchange got serious…very quickly.

There was something that drew me very close to him, and it was not physical. It was more. It was his eyes. His eyes told me that he was in a lot of pain. I knew the pain, and I wanted to help ease him. His eyes shimmered with betrayal.

His eyes were so penetrating that when I stared for more than a minute, a sense of wonder took place in me, almost like when one stares at the ocean searching for answers, for whys. That look haunted me for so long. That look is why I waited for him to return to me; he'd forgotten about love and love's name.

Time passed, and I sensed that he was running from something; I couldn't put my finger on it. I surmised it was a fear of commitment. There were so many times when I caught him staring at me with the same wonder that took place in me, but in that "wonder," he feared something. Intuitively, I knew that it was more than just being hurt.

Like everything else in my happy-chaotic life, good things must come to an end. For some time before he forgot about love, things were a bit rocky. Confusion set in. I was confused about whether this relationship was it or if he was it. Albeit this relationship was everything I wanted. It was mature, fun, loving, and we connected spiritually. We were friends, lovers, and all that makes for a great love story.

I was grappling with moving in with another man who was not my child's father. Nonetheless, the thought that I would have to bring another man into my children's lives was not something I desired. I knew he was a great man; he loved my children, and my children loved him. He saw life and a future with me, with them, and yet, I feared that my children would resent me because children always prefer to have daddy at home. It was mom's guilt or sabotage, probably both.

As a Latina, I was mortified by what my family (by family, I mean what my mother) was going to say.

In the Latino culture, especially in families with a strong religious background, it is frowned upon for women to go from men to men, especially after having children. According to my mother, I was supposed to wait seven years before I engaged in any kind of relationship with any other man because the bible said so. I had to point out to my mother that this scenario was specific to widows, and since my children's dads were alive, I was not about to uphold that tradition! My mother said, "You just don't learn, do you? Por eso es que te pasan las cosas." As if things happened to me because I purposely sought after them—shit happens to everybody, everywhere, and every day!

There were other factors as well. My "Science Project" wanted so much. He wanted three kids, and I wanted no more (somewhere during the relationship, he reduced it to one—tan lindo, compromising). It became another hurdle for us. I knew I did not want any more children; I also did not want to take the experience of being a father away from him. Staying with him would be misleading, and I knew I would not change my mind.

He wanted a stay-at-home mom. Although enticing in theory, and I must admit that I contemplated it many times, the reality was different. I have been working since the age of thirteen, and as a Capricorn, much of my life revolved around making a better life for myself, including being financially free. I would not be able to function just as a stay-at-home mom. While constantly bitching that I need a break from work and I need to stay home, that is the biggest lie I can tell anyone.

I enjoy being productive. What better productivity than being a mom twenty-four-hour? You may ask. It is beautiful to have the ability to be with your children all the time, but I just couldn't (I wrote this in 2007. I've changed my mind since.)

It was fear. Fear of being bound financially to a man.

To top it all off, he wanted to relocate to Florida or Arizona---I don't think so! Just thinking about the name Arizona makes me dry and thirsty. Although I come from a Tropical Island, 105 degrees is an exaggeration.

I'm a New Yorker. I love this chaotic city life and its wild, stubborn, self-centered, entitled, yet endearing, and passionate eight million people. I love its four seasons (though I'm always complaining about the noise, the dirt, the cold, the heat). I love that there's always a beat on the streets. One can go anywhere at any time of the day or night and find people - you're never alone in New York City. Arizona—pleeease!

I have a love-hate relationship with this crazy city called New York. It's a beautiful love affair, and I did not want to give that up (I told you that I love with limitations).

It wasn't so much leaving New York that I was resisting. Underneath it all was - fear. I was terrified that he was just a dream. Fear that it might be true. Fear of being happy. Fear of not feeling worthy of all the joy he brought me. Everything was moving so fast yet so perfect, but the slow tethering of fear crippled me.

He also had many issues to deal with when it came to women. He had a mother wound. Like me, he also dealt with betrayal. The women in his past had destroyed him, and in turn, he shattered other innocent women. He feared that this would catch up to him—it would.

That kept me from taking the next step in my relationship with my Science Project. I was still healing from childhood issues, teenage-hood issues, womanhood issues. Issues around morality, society, and its expectations of a twenty-something-year-old with two children, a single parent going to school full-time, working full time, a daughter, sister, and friend. Issues around forgiveness, self-love, love for others, resentment, and redemption.

My Science Project had a way of making me understand that he was here to stay. He repeatedly reminded me that he came to simplify my life. I could see his devotion to me, my kids, our future, and us in every action.

He would pick me up after a night of dancing, no matter what time; it did not matter if he was sleeping or at work doing a double shift. He hated the idea that something could happen to me and not being able to protect me. He would show up with my favorite roses just because I was having a bad day, or because I was happy, or just because - he didn't need reasons; he only wanted to make me smile. He always told me that even my name bore royalty; therefore, he would treat me as such royalty; hence, his nickname for me was "Princesita." He wrote me cards and love letters and dedicated songs to me, to us, to love. Every moment I spent with him superseded the last. He would stop the car abruptly to show me the moon or sun or take me to remote locations in New York City that I had taken for granted just to absorb the beauty, the mystery, and the majesty that is New York.

He reinvented our story in every moment. There was a closeness, a deep level of intimacy (not just sexually) we were developing that I had not experienced until he came into my life.

Everything, well not everything, almost everything I have said I would not do - I had done, and a lot of what I had planned to do had yet to manifest. I had spat up in the air and salivated all over myself (That taught me not to spit in the air). I had judged so many people who, in turn, judged me.

Over time, change is bound to occur, and sometimes, events in your life mark you or, better yet, affect you to such depths - that the person you were - becomes extinct..., sometimes for the better - sometimes, for the worse.

But some scars do not let you live, dream, or move forward. There are wounds so powerful that they dominate every move and thought. Some scars can be traced by every laughter, cry, or act; some wounds are so deep that bringing someone else to share them with becomes the source of your destruction; your thoughts become the phantoms that will scare away any sign of light. Some scars, even with time, don't get close to healing.

My Science Project was that light, that angel that came to help ease my wounds, but I feared me, my scars, my vulnerability.

Let's face it, I was afraid of LOVE.

What I knew of romantic love up until that point, was that it was abusive, painful, and served with never ending platter of betrayals.

Life has a plan for you that may not be in accord with the plans you have set out for yourself; whenever this happens, life creates a life-altering event to provide an opportunity to realign yourself with its plan, and if you still choose otherwise, destruction follows.

The years of abuse had hardened and putrefied me in a way, but he was patient. He insisted that there was a freer version of me under all that pain, hurt, and toughness. He often begged me to let that version out, to free myself from exhaustion, bondage, and loneliness.

84

It was challenging for me to be close, but he brought out the best in me; I found it easy to be soft around him. He taught me to slow down and to appreciate his life and physical touch which I craved so much in life but feared it since childhood.

I became accustomed to rough hands and harsh treatment. I had experienced hands that took without permission, thus making "touch" a trigger. But his hands were baby-soft, as if untouched by life; his hands felt like silk to my body and, more importantly, to my soul. It felt like talc powder on my face whenever he touched me. *He taught me that kisses seal. Kisses uplift. Kisses, he said, "heal."*

I surrendered to love. I submitted to my Science Project, to his love, but my past was lurking, dictating my present. My "Science Project" reminded me of life before him and what life with him could be if I chose to be his forever. Once, he asked me, "What did I fear most, my past or him not being in my life at all?" When I began to see a world without him, I saw misery, loneliness, and despondency. I saw long walks lost inside myself. I saw barren streets 365 days a year, as if his absence interrupted standard weather patterns and left me only with winter. I saw love waving its last goodbye and telling me in that 'goodbye letter' that she (love) was not returning because I did not appreciate her. I understood at that moment that I could not live in fear anymore. Realizing that my life without him did not make sense. I surrendered.

Surrendering to him, to his promises gave me power. I felt invincible. For once, I felt that all the pieces of my life came together. I decided to be happy. To bask in him. To block out every voice of doubt, the voice of pain, and to trust the present. He filled my nights with hope and an abundance unknown to me. I decided to enjoy those eyes that captivated my soul to the point of surrender. I decided to enjoy his soft hands caressing me instead of beating me. I chose to enjoy conversations about plans, yes, even Arizona! I was in complete bliss, the kind of bliss aligned with the

85

meeting of stars and planets. I was in a state of transcendence until reality brought me back to a painful truth: *Some love stories, and all great love stories, must face the big test...*

will the Science Project remember love?

Shit!
I Hate the Dark

I have always feared the dark, the night, and what lurks in the unseen, perhaps because my earlier memories of the dark were so traumatizing. Fear took hold of me when I opened my eyes and saw darkness. I heard speeding cars; Something had just happened, and it was terrible.

I realized we had a car accident. I looked to my right and left, and my Science Project was not there. I began calling his name as loud as I could. It hurt my bones whenever I yelled, but I kept calling out for him to no avail. I wanted to get up; I was fighting my body, but I couldn't, as if it had cemented to the grass. I was losing my mind, and fear began to kiss me.

Two good Samaritans came to my aid. They called the ambulance; the wife seemed horrified. I assumed she had witnessed the accident; she gave me her cell phone. I called my mom. I was bleeding and scared. All I could think of was to ask my mom to pray. EMTs could not find My Science Project. I told them not to give up that he was out there.

The paramedics finally found him and seemed petrified by what they found. My Science Project and I got air-lifted in separate helicopters to the hospital. I kept asking if he was alive. They did not answer. They kept telling me "He was getting the best care and to focus on me." Insensitive. How could I focus on me? Did they not know - I love this man! That our story just begun? How could I focus on myself if he was injured, lifeless? How, if I am not by his side and unable to hold his hand, tell him I love him? They insisted that I try to calm down and ask questions I did not know the answer to. All I remembered was that he was allergic to Penicillin. I was so confused. All I could remember was him asking me about "life without him." At that moment, I realized how much I wanted to do life with him.

I was in the emergency room praying, praying, and crying. I missed his eyes, the intensity he projected when he looked at me. I missed that fire, that look of innocence, fear, pain, sense of loss, protection. Almost as if I knew I would never see them again.

That one night, so many promises and dreams and our hopeful future became questioned marked. My Science Project would undergo two brain, liver, and lung surgeries in one night. "No chance of life," the doctors said. Nothing was told to me, and no one had an answer. Survivor's guilt set in, the 'why me?' began, and all I could think of was, had we arrived at our destination?

The novela begins!

Eternal Wait

The worst feeling is waiting- it is not human-like. Human beings are not programmed to wait because waiting requires patience, a skill only attained from facing lots of adversity. I like to be in control.

The word 'wait' implies the exact opposite of that. It means the situation is not within my reach or control; I cannot change nor affect its outcome. The control factor is removed when one must wait, and desperation sets in.

I did not see him for two days, and there was no answer. Everything was *waiting*. The only information trickling in was that he was in critical condition and that I should *wait*. The thoughts that ran through my head were outrageous. My physical pain increased with each idea as it provoked the sedation to go away.

I was saddened by the thought that he was in pain or suffering, and I could do nothing to alleviate him. That I could lose him, precisely now, that I had finally surrendered and decided to be happy with him, and now, he may not be around to enjoy our future. I was in pain, but it was more than physical; it was my heart. My soul could not contain itself, and nothing calmed me. I just wanted to be brought to his side to care for him.

I saw him on the third day after the accident. My initial reaction was to cry in pure disbelief at what I saw. I took a deep breath and composed myself. He did not look like himself. The hematoma caused his brain to swell to what seemed at least three sizes. Bandages covered his head; endless machines and tubes attached to his body, the life support machine beeping away, and my Love looked lifeless on that bed. I felt the floor beneath me implode, and despair hugged me.

The cruelty of that moment, how surreal and untimely. Why was he in that bed, fighting for life, not speaking, not responding, not aware, in a coma? I wanted to

89

think that moment was not real; it could not be. Why at this moment? He didn't deserve this. We didn't deserve this. Our story had just started; we had plans, so much to do, and so many promises to realize, and now all is on hold. I held his hands, and they felt so cold; I wanted my warmth to miraculously warm him out of that coma and get him up from that bed.   That coldness in his hands made me understand the fragility of it all, the fragility of life. The frailty of love.

I paid attention to every beep in those machines; I needed to make sure that there were signs of life. Every beep was scarier than the previous. I could not contain my sorrow and began weeping, the way one cries when someone you love goes away forever.

The following day, the staff allowed me to see him again, ensuring I kept my composure. This time, it was just me and him in the room. A male nurse entered the room. I looked at him, and he saw my pain. He said, "he will be okay; just believe." I guess he wanted to console me.

I held his hand again, and as I squeezed it, his right eye opened. He opened his eyes and mouth as if attempting to tell me something, but he didn't. I asked the nurse if this was a sign, and he assured me it wasn't and probably just a reflex and not something he intended to do. To me, it was a sign that my Science Project was communicating from the depth of his sleep, that he heard me and was saying: "He was okay, that he was going to be okay, to remain strong and faithful, to hold on to him, to our story, to our love, and that he loved me."

Holding his hands, I realized how much I missed his voice, calling me "Princesita " or "Dominicanita"—telling me he was crazy about me. I remembered the first time he confessed he loved me at the Dyckman Marina on Thanksgiving Day. His nervousness as he confessed, he loved me. His voice replayed in my mind; the way a scratched vinyl record repeatedly replays when the needle gets stuck. My needle was stuck on him saying, "he loved me", and the more I heard the recording of his voice replaying, the more I missed him, and suddenly a real sense of loss set in me. When I realized I might not hear his voice for a while, I became obsessed with remembering it. I cannot count how many times I replayed the voicemail messages he had left me. The only things I had to hold on to him were our memories and his voice; that kept me close to him and brought me comfort. I replayed our relationship over and over in my head. It's incredible how the human mind will attach in fear that memory may become extinct. That's what I did. I stuck to our memories like Crazy Glue, the same way a child clings to her mother when she's about to leave for a prolonged period.

I realized I had taken his voice for granted, like children take their parents for granted, assuming they will always be around. I took for granted his kindness, his gentleness. I took his jokes and cynical views for granted. The way he caressed my body, his instinctual thirst for me. I thought about how much time it took me to recognize our moment. To recognize us. That realization made me feel worse.

I felt alone, although I was never alone. I once read in a book that *"Solitude is not being lonely; solitude is being where you're not even at,"* and I understood this. I was not present. Physically, my body was on earth, in that hospital, in that lonely hotel room, in the airplane, but my mind..., my mind was elsewhere. I wasn't anywhere I was in. I was in that coma state with him. I was lost in the eternities of infinity, for I saw where infinity and eternity met. I was lost in dreams, remembrance, space, atoms, and molecules; I was lost with my Science Project; I was where he was.

All I could do was cry and pray. I believed in us and the love we had for one another. I knew that no matter how bad this situation was- God wouldn't start anything he did not intend to finish. While this situation seemed to be the ending of our love story, it appeared that it had just begun.

His vitals kept rising as I held his hands and spoke to him.   Almost as if he were telling me that he understood. That he was fighting, that he would fight until the very end. I began praying over him, for us, and he started calming down.

Some prayers are never answered.

Family Matters

His family began walking into the room; I greeted everyone I had met before the accident and was introduced to those I had not yet met. I knew of everyone by reference to my Science Project.

Before the accident, he and I had been planning a gathering to have our families formally meet, and it would take place upon returning from this trip. We took this trip to introduce each other to our friends who lived in the Sunshine State.

He had set a few days before the accident. However, I kept postponing because I was afraid. I feared his family would not accept me since I had children, and he had none. Many Latino families oppose a man getting involved with a woman with children. I feared he would feel pressured to end the relationship if his family did not accept me. He was the traditional independent-dependent Latino man close to his family, but I knew he wouldn't have allowed interference.

That is why 'fear' is so powerful. I understood that what he felt for me was strong enough that he wouldn't abandon me, but fear overruled me. At the core, I did not want everyone to meet because part of me wanted to keep him all to myself without the intrusion of others. I did not want anyone interfering in the way we did things. I did not want to share him with his family or mine.

His father walked in and hugged me affectionately as he always did. More family members entered the room, and his sister, whom I had not met, was the last to enter. I extended my hand to greet her. She barely responded. Lilly was her name.

I don't know if I was overly sensitive or heavily medicated, but I sensed hatred from her. It was palpable! I felt as if she slapped me without any hands. She walked by me, and an eerie feeling took place in me. Her eyes were the bleakest eyes I had ever seen. They were intense, bordering

93

on evil. I immediately ruled out the thought, as you attract what you think. I began telling myself that she was engulfed in pain. She was distraught, and understandably so. She practically raised my "Science Project," and he simply loved her as a mother figure. The moment was too much for me, and I returned to my room.

I was discharged from the hospital the following day and headed to say good night to my Science Project before leaving. Lilly and the others were with him and about to leave as well.

As I was leaving, his dad asked me if "I wanted to stay with them in the hotel?" I said I did not want to impose. He insisted, but gently, I declined. Lilly offered me a ride to the nearest hotel, and I agreed.

As we're exiting the hospital, Lilly says, "I see that you came out of the accident untouched. I heard you had at least some broken bones, but I see now that is not true". I did not know how to respond to such a statement. I couldn't say, "well, thank God, Lilly. I walked out untouched while my boyfriend-your brother is dying, or better yet, "you seemed unhappy that I did not break any—bitch."
I opted to look at her with eyes that expressed, "I know what you're doing".

She proceeded to offer me money. I politely declined, for she was not offering money out of kindness; she was offering me money as a statement, a position of power, and I let her know that I had money. I saw how she looked at me from the rearview mirror, which made me cringe.

I did not sleep that night; I just cried and tossed in the bed. I had sedatives that did not sedate. I could not bear the thought that my Science Project was in grave danger while I was in that hotel room. Him, alone in that hospital room, and I could not be beside him, giving him strength, supporting him, telling him that I loved him.

94

Shit...,
Waiting Rooms are Interrogation Rooms

I endured the night and headed to the hospital. On the way to the cafeteria, I coincided with Lilly. Trying to break the ice, I told her that my Science Project spoke highly of her. He loved her very much, and while it was unfortunate to meet her under these circumstances, I was glad to have met her since she meant so much to him. She began crying, saying that "he was like her son. That she practically raised him." She expressed how proud of him she was, and now his life was over. I reminded her that he was a strong man and a fighter and would come out of this—better and stronger. She looked at me for the first time with soft, hopeful, and loving eyes.

Everyone gathered in the Waiting Room, and it wasn't long before Lilly began asking questions about the accident. I explained that I did not remember much from the accident. I had fallen asleep after an asthmatic episode. The last thing I remembered was My Science Project waking me up to ask me if I wanted anything from the store. I replied, "No," and fell back to sleep. I woke up after the accident had taken place. I said, "I was so sorry and wished I had been in that bed instead of My Science Project. Almost everyone said "No"! to that statement except for Lilly, almost as if agreeing with my wishes.

Gloria, my Science Project's best friend, was the first person to arrive at the hospital after receiving the call about the accident. She visited me the entire time I was hospitalized. She was very sweet. Naturally, I grew close to her. I was grateful that although we'd never met, I guess out of loyalty to my Science Project, she visited me while visiting him.

Gloria asked for my children, which confounded Lilly.

She interjected:

"You have two kids"!

She wanted everyone in that hospital to know I wasn't pure or fit to be her brother's girlfriend.

The realization that I had two children made her disdain for me grow deeper. I realized then that my fears about meeting the rest of his family were valid. The problem is not that she disliked me but that she began recruiting others to see me as an enemy. Insecure and weak people are like that- they cannot hate you on their own merit. They must ruin you. Soon after, some of her siblings began treating me in ways they hadn't before, and the tension expanded like wildfire. I began to feel the heaviness of being in a place where *I was not accepted, wanted, or loved.*

While waiting for visiting hours to start, I noticed Lilly pacing back and forth. The nurse came in to inform us that it was okay to see him, but only three people at a time. Everyone got up at the same time. Lilly immediately said, "Family first." His father held my hands and brought me in. He suggested I not pay too much attention to Lilly as sometimes, "she gets out of hand." At this point, I understood that my intuition was accurate and that this journey would be an uphill battle.

Inside the room, I could barely hold or speak to him. Shortly after, the neurologist entered the room to speak about the brain injury recovery process and what can be expected. He had two booklets on how families can cope with each phase of the recovery process. He gave one to me and one to his father. Lilly's eyes could not emit any more hate. I gave her the book as I wanted to diffuse the situation. The doctor immediately sensed the tension and began speaking about the importance of staying together for the sake of the patient and that all who could contribute to his progress needed to do it in their respective ways. He also told me that he would bring me a book since I was involved in the accident, and as his girlfriend, I would need to know how to deal with my boyfriend's recovery process. Lilly was fuming; it must have bruised her ego to know that everyone knew who he and I were, and she would have to accept it one way or another.

It was cumbersome to deal with the agonizing pain that my Science Project was battling, life and death, and to have to deal with the nonsensical behavior of some of his siblings was another battle I did not want to partake in. I have never felt so much hate in the name of love. I did not cry. As a matter of fact, the more they hated me, the more support I offered, and the stronger I appeared.

Life unfolds as it always does, and my responsibilities back home were calling. I left for New York and flew back to Florida every other week until the argument with Lilly (You remember in the beginning I told you that every love story has a few evil bitches and villains that make the story more complex. You didn't think this one was any different-did you?)

Yes, Lilly was his sister, but she thought she owned my Science Project. Some women raise children or siblings to be the husbands they never had or wished they had. Some raise them to think that they belong to them. She ensured my days were a complete hell in the following weeks and months.

As if having him lifeless on that bed wasn't enough, this woman wanted to make me feel I was the reason the accident happened. She would not allow me any alone time with him; she went as far as asking a family friend to investigate pressing legal charges against me.

My Science Project came out of the coma two months after the accident. I immediately booked a flight to see him. He had woken up from the coma but was not responsive, didn't speak, didn't move, and lost his memory.

I was in the room with him when Lilly entered. She barely acknowledged me but proceeded to tell me he had a tough night and thought he would die. I felt terrible and wanted to console her, even though she was not kind to me. I know that she loved him very much and that she too was in pain over her brother; that's why I tried to understand her behavior. I wanted to justify her hate and put myself in her shoes. It was probably hard to see me, someone she'd just met under these circumstances. Her beloved brother was in a coma and seeing me walking free of harm must have been devastating. Nevertheless, I could not understand this because, if she knew her brother at all, she would have intuited that he would never be alright, knowing that any harm came to me or anyone else under his watch. It would have crushed his spirit, more importantly, what kind of person wishes another harm?

Lilly exited the room to make a phone call; Gloria and I stayed with him. Although he had woken up from the coma, he was delicate. He had a trachea that served as a feeding tube. He had so much phlegm; every time he coughed, one had to insert a tube to extract the phlegm. He was weak and so different from the man I took that trip with. His frame did not resemble the chiseled body I knew. He had lost a significant amount of weight. A man full of life, hopes, and dreams looked like he was withering away.

I did not know what to say to him or if it was appropriate to touch him because he appeared enfeebled. A nurse came in and saw my ambivalence and reaffirmed that it was okay to touch and speak to him, encourage him even, so long as he did not get agitated.

"Love is All" by Marc Anthony came to my mind as I held his hand (It was one of our favorite songs). Lilly came into the room, and I'm assuming that my humming a song irritated the devil in her. She got on her knees pleading with me to "leave him alone, to not kill him." I was dumbfounded, clearly, this woman was insane!

I tried to explain to her that the nurse reassured me that it was okay to speak to him, but she did not let me say a word. She became erratic and hysterical! She went on a rant about how I would have to get used to having a bunch of women coming in and out. That I was not the only one, that there were others, that he had been lying to me all this time. That there was nothing special between him and me, that he promised others the same.

As the information entered my ears, I tried to rule out what was truth from fiction. I thought this woman was irate; she would say anything to get me to leave. I did not want to create a scene, so I told her "That I was leaving out of respect for him, but the day would come when his memory returned, and she would have to answer him as to why I was not next to him" and left.

I did not see him for three weeks after the neurotic episode with his sister. I journaled about him every day, I cried for him, and I became obsessed with looking at his picture; It was my way of holding on to him, as a piece of me disintegrated with every day that I did not see him.

I threw myself into my work and motherly duties to not think of my sadness.

The thing about distracting yourself from your pain..., that pain is present in everything you do, in everything you don't say, and in every emotion you don't feel. It's there, in the coffee you pretend to enjoy, in the hope the next breath is easier..., it is always there prowling like a coyote in the distance.

For eight hours of the day, work became a filler for the pain I was avoiding; at the time I was a Case Manager for the victims of 911 and Flight 587, and I felt impotent as my participants would tell me their problems, and I wanted to tell them mine. I just sat there not fully present, seeing my Science Project in everything they said, in their agony. At times, I felt compelled to have my cases transferred over because I knew that it was not fair to my participants. They too were dealing with horrible events, grief, despair, and mounting despair in their lives.

I tried to find solace in the ability to help them navigate such traumatizing experiences, hoping in turn that this would validate my pain. It didn't. A part of me felt that I was cheating on my Science Project by working and dealing. Then home. The children, the questions, the homework, bedtime. I felt awful for my children because adulthood is a stage that remains until we die, but childhood is brief, it will never come back. There I am, the person responsible for ensuring that my children had a good childhood, and I was the first to ruin it for them. I would try to explain that mommy was sad, but children don't understand sadness or pain, they just want to play. I hugged them, hugged them tightly. I tried playing with them, but I became frustrated because of the noise that they made. I

100

forced myself. I couldn't wait for them to go to sleep so that I could cry.

That's the thing about motherhood: women have been conditioned to think that mothers don't have a license to feel and experience real emotion because the expectation is that you're a mother first, a human being second, and a woman last.

My nights were long, incredibly lonely, and painful; crying became part of my nighttime repertoire. Sadly, I found pleasure in thinking about him, crying for him (It's how I purge energy).

Every moment without him made me feel the cold and bold winter that undertook the city that year. When one is in love, winter is romantic and hoped for. The idea of rolling down a hill covered in white or just staying indoors drinking a hot cup of cocoa while cuddling is very enticing, but winter, apart from your love, is gloomy and insufferable.

The frigid air penetrates the soul, and one becomes as frigid as the air itself. According to meteorologists, New York had not seen a colder winter in a hundred years. It was the kind of cold that hugged your entire being and paralyzed all movements and thoughts.

I would lay in my bed and wonder if he "sensed me" even though he had lost his memory. If the blueprint of 'us' was still etched in his soul. If he sensed my suffering, my cries, or if he even knew that I was alive. If he remembered love.

I couldn't contain the distance, and after three weeks, I booked a flight on a limb, not knowing whether I could see him, but I didn't care. I would chance it- even if I saw him from afar. I got to the hospital without being noticed. I did not know how he was going to react. I walked in, and he was lying down with eyes that were wondering where they were, the way infants and children wonder when they go to an unfamiliar place, trying to decipher it.

I said "hello", but he did not respond. I mentioned my name, and he did not respond. My heart began to beat faster and faster. I wanted to cry but did not. A physical therapist entered the room. I introduced myself and told him with teary eyes that My Science Project did not remember me. He told me "it was expected and that it would take him a while." I stared at him, hoping that he would recognize my eyes, to no avail.

The inevitable happened: The phone rang. I had to pick up. If I didn't, the therapist would notice my ambivalence and call me on it. It would be suspicious that I was next to the phone and hesitated to pick it up. What to do? I picked up the phone, and lo and behold- it was my Science Project's girlfriend (I know you're raising your eyebrows now saying "What!" wondering who this is? Remember, every novela has a few antagonists throughout the story).

Sandy is a girl claiming she had been with my Science for seven or eight years. When I returned to New York after the accident, I called the hotel where his dad and Lilly stayed to find out about My Science Project progress. To my demise, Sandy picked up the phone.
Wondering who she was, I asked "who I was speaking with. I apologized for not recognizing the voice and stated that while in the hospital, I was heavily sedated and to please forgive me."
Sandy responded, "We have never met. My name is Sandy, his girlfriend of seven or eight years." I said, "excuse me? I'm sorry, could you repeat yourself?"
"I am his girlfriend."

At this point, I was stunned but could not bring myself to hang up. I wanted to know more.
She continued, "this is not the first time he has cheated on me".
"Huh?"
"Quite frankly, I'm tired of his cheating".
I absorbed as much information as my heart and brain could process.

102

"He told me about this trip. I know he was here. He told me we would speak when he got back to New York".

I finally responded, "it took eleven days for you to see your boyfriend of seven years?"

"His family asked me not to come over since you were here."

The story was not adding up to me.

I followed up with "why would you take into consideration a stranger when your man of seven years- the man you love is in a bed dying?"
"I respect his family."

I wasn't satisfied with the answer, so I kept probing her, "when did you two last see each other?"
"Valentine's weekend".

As she finished that sentence, a sudden relief set in me, as he and we had spent a glorious Valentine's weekend together. I decided to stand by him. He was still in a coma when this conversation took place, and, under those circumstances, I could not decide, nor could he defend himself, for that matter. I was not about to accuse him without allowing him to clear his name, and Sandy did not enjoy this at all. She warned me of doomsday and all the pain and suffering he would put me through. I did not have the energy or desire to lend her an ear. I apologized on his behalf (women do this often, apologizing for things they have no business apologizing for) and hung up the phone.

Sandy called the room. I immediately passed the phone to my Science Project after giving her my name. She was furious and threatened to call his father and family and tell them I was there. It enraged her that I was by his side.
The phone rang again; this time, it was Lilly's daughter, whom I never met or interacted with prior to this call yet hated me (like mother-like daughter). She asked, "how I got by security."

103

I thought to myself, I'm sorry—I didn't know I was a fugitive, a wanted criminal, or a terrorist; last time I checked, I was an abiding citizen.

I responded, "What do you mean by how I got by security? It's not as if the front desk has my picture and a caption that reads, wanted".

Five minutes elapsed, and the nurse apologized beforehand and asked me to leave the premises, escorting me to the elevator door to ensure I left. This was infuriating, humiliating, and disheartening. Not only did my Science Project not recognize me, but I was also being treated like a criminal for fun.

The thought that he could come out of this thinking that I abandoned him was torturous to me. He would never find out what I endured just to be by his side.

Destiny was showing me the other side of its face and doing everything possible to separate us.

Sandy became my nemesis. We had never met, but I knew she was dangerous. She had access to him and his family.

She could manipulate his memory loss to her advantage, like in novelas. She could say that she was his wife, his girlfriend, that it was she he loved, that they lived together, all those things kept haunting my mind.

I had an advantage over her, though, I believed in love. I believed he loved me, and that kept me going. He connected with me on a deep level. He liked who I was when I was with him and away from him. We were friends, we were lovers, and we were in love. Although he had lost his memory, there was something about what we had that was going to help him connect the dots. I knew that he would respond to me sooner or later. There was a force from within that would tell him that "I was special to him," even if he could not label it as love, but that connection would lead him back to me from wherever his mind was. I knew that infinity was not distant enough, that my prayers and thoughts would catch up with his mind.

I knew that no matter what alliances Sandy formed with his family and friends, what mattered was what he had to say at the end of the day. I just hoped that it would be soon.

He was no longer in a coma. I was confident that at one point, he was going to ask for me, and they (family and friends) would have to answer. They could manipulate the situation to favor them, but time would prevail, and our story would be vindicated. I was hoping I was right.

Despite the morning's embarrassment, I knew I couldn't give up on my attempts to see my Science Project before heading back to New York City. I grew ovaries and tried my luck again. I placed a call to the rehabilitation center, and, to my surprise, his father answered the phone and asked me to join him. I embraced the opportunity and went to the hospital immediately.

I was there next to him, and it was bliss. He recognized me and stated my full name. I asked him do you remember me? And he nodded yes; I asked him who I was, and he replied, "My girlfriend." To hear his voice brought me to an elated state. It had been months since I heard his raspy voice- let alone him uttering my name. Hearing my name from his mouth felt like peace had embraced me again.

For the first time in months, my heart felt normal. The skies opened at that moment and hearing him say it with such conviction was like having an orgasm. What excited me was that he said it in front of family members. A part of me felt vindicated, as if part of the battle was won (far from it, I would later find out).

But that moment was indescribable for me. For the first time in weeks, I smiled openly, and all the cells in my body felt recharged and revived. It was a huge step; he cheated death, he beat the coma, and, in his amnesia, he managed to remember me. He did love me. I was important to him. He remembered me. He remembered love.

He began grabbing me, asking me to join him in bed. He held my face and stroked his hand through my long black hair- feeling its texture, wondering when and where he had touched it. He wanted me then and there in front of everyone. He was oblivious to bystanders.

My blood pressure started to rise. I had waited weeks for this- for his touch, for him to desire me the way he did before the accident. My body always felt prey to his touch, and this time was no different. My body was tingling all over, the same sensation I felt every time we kissed—this desperate need to be with him whenever he wanted me.

My breasts reacted to his requests as he touched me. I wanted to give him all of me, make him remember how it used to be, how the bed was our hellfire. How passionate and different we made it every time. I wanted to place my neck on his lips to see what he would do, knowing instinctively, he would begin biting and nibbling around the ear. As I try to take off my shirt and place my brown areolas in his mouth, hoping to trigger his memory to remember how they fed his desires once upon a time. To have him remember how lost he became with them.

I hoped he mustered enough strength to lift my skirt and have his fingers locate the passages of passion he regularly conquered. Have him find that spot that brought me before his mercy as he teased me until I began purring like a kitty needing affection. I didn't. I couldn't.

I was not sure if this outpouring of lust resulted from his damaged brain, and he regressed to his infancy. If was his mother he wanted, or if, indeed, he automatically remembered passion. I knew it wasn't the latter. I relaxed him as much as I could and, in the process, tried to calm myself.

As I caressed his face, I noticed the receding side of his face. His frontal lobe bone was removed and placed in his liver during the initial brain surgery to allow the swelling in the brain to subside, thus avoiding additional trauma to the brain and/or death.

I did not want to overwhelm him, so I reiterated how proud I was of him, how much I missed him, and that I looked forward to having him back home.

It was tear-jerking to see him struggling to do things he could do effortlessly before. While every step in his recovery was monumental for everyone who cared for him, it was hard, nonetheless. Seeing him battle to execute essential functions, such as getting up to no avail, was a hard pill to swallow.

There is so much we take for granted in life, and tragic events like these wake us up to the reality we ignore: how blessed we are to execute daily tasks and body parts functioning correctly, only to push them when they do not function properly or at all.

His voice, which had such vibrato, was now frail, child-like, and low in tempo. After laying in that bed for many months, his plumped and nectarous lips were chapped and pale. His beautiful, monolid brown eyes were still wandering. I could tell he was trying to remember everything but could not.

Holding his hands, I closed my eyes and praised God for the miracle he performed. I was confident that he would recuperate fully from his amnesia. I asked God to help me be an instrument of his love in his recovery.

Back In New York City

I returned to New York City, hopeful and trusting that this situation would resolve itself.

Shortly after that, he was transferred to a rehabilitation center in New York. He made enormous progress; his speech was more expansive, and while partially confined to a wheelchair, his motor skills improved, and he was more alert.

He'd managed to memorize my phone number and would call me daily at four p.m., maintaining part of our routine before the accident.

Despite his condition, he continued to inspire me. Here he was dealing with one of the most trying situations a human being can endure. Yet, he remained positive (there are lots of highs and lows with brain injury recovery patients), relentless, challenging himself to get better even when he did not feel like it. I admired that in him, his tenacity and thirst for life.

He was remembering love, and by him remembering, he continued to teach me about hope and about love.

The Great Dilemma
Time can heal or open wounds!

Inner strength requires us to go within and assess ourselves thoroughly, and account for the emotional and spiritual reservoir to address issues as they arise. Life's challenges and difficulties often cloud our vision because the problem seems insurmountable, the process intimidating, and the solution out of reach, even if it stares us in the face.

I am emotionally strong, tenacious, and resilient. Seldom do I give up in any situation. I always come out on top, even when I feel like I'm drowning. I can power through uncomfortable situations by diminishing my circumstances, convincing myself that *'it can always be worse and/or that there is someone else that has a greater obstacle than me.'* This method may seem counterintuitive since one must honor what one feels to heal. However, some moments are action-driven, and others that require introspection.

The weight of this situation, with its myriad emotional, psychological, and spiritual moving parts, felt like spiritual warfare. I couldn't foretell the outcome and was beginning to question whether it would favor me. It required more patience than I could withstand; between my Science Project process, memory loss, and feud with his family, I began losing trust in my ability to sustain this situation in the name of love.

Throughout his recovery, more women began visiting him; most introduced themselves as ex-girlfriends, but the insecurity about where he and I stood began invading my thoughts. Moreover, Sandy had become a hemorrhoid to my existence.

My inner voice was a in incessant battle between logic and the heart. My intuition told me that his siblings, mainly (Lilly and one of his brothers) were creating unnecessary drama, hoping our relationship would end, forcing me to leave his life for good. Logic and what seemed the most plausible possibility was that my beloved

Science Project had been lying to me all along. I wanted to give him the benefit of the doubt, a fair trial, but I couldn't. He had lost most of his memory.

If left unattended, the mind will wander to unimaginable lengths to drive one crazy. The ego works overtime to protect itself from being hurt. It enraged me when I thought about the possibility of him lying to me throughout our relationship. I felt betrayed and naïve. Tolerating degrading and dehumanizing behaviors from his loved ones just to be next to him, loyal as a dog. Defending his honor against all odds, going against the current all the while, he'd dishonored our story. I began begrudging him and the situation. Beneath it all, I resented myself.

I was at a forked road; do I stay or leave him? Grappling with whether to allow destiny to reunite us years later or stay to fight a good battle in the name of love. Could I stay loyal to our story without any answers? What if he never fully remembers? Reality was slapping me with the fact that if I stayed, I would have to stay without answers, without questioning his betrayal and what we were trying to build. I would have to forgive a transgression I may or may never verify. I would have to forget about all those revelations. was I equipped to even do that?

Betrayal is insidious. It strips one of logic and reason, it does not care about love, about time spent. Betrayal only looks to honor the anger, the rage, and restitution for the wrongdoing. How can one go through life not defining things if everything about life is a definition? I need to feel in control, and defining things, events, and people gives me that clarity.

I have spent most of my life defining who I am as a citizen, person, daughter, mother, and everything under the sun. But I wanted to do things differently with him. I wanted to go with the flow with him. I wanted to stop being a Doubting Thomas and trust that this "love story" was beautiful and worth letting it unfold as God intended.

Reality was setting in, and all my fears came true. The man I had defended for so long, the dream I was living, was falling apart before me. I saw love diluting as the minutes passed. It seemed as if everything was a lie.

All these women and their love stories about my Science Project, the glorious times spent the funny and sad times. I just sat there listening to them tell their stories as if I were their fucking counselor. All the while, Marc Anthony's song is playing in the background. Outwardly, I looked calm, but inwardly - I was fuming. I looked at my Science Project with both love and disdain. Hearing these women sing along to our songs, *Marc Anthony's* songs. The songs that spoke to each of the stages we went through, as if we were in a concert, and not a rehabilitation center..., with a man that owed me an explanation!

Music inspires and heals me; I make myself the song's protagonist while losing myself in it until whatever is happening is gone. Just me and the song, the plot, the voice, the artist. Marc Anthony was ours. We loved him. I have always loved Marc Anthony. I love how he sings; he sings as though every song is the last song he will ever sing. I love that. I connect to that passion.

The *Libre* album was meant for us, as if God directed the composers to write our love story. That CD went with us everywhere; we played it in the car, at work, at his house. It was us. Even in his amnesia, *Libre* was still speaking to our love story.

As the concert in his room continued, I wondered whether my Science Project knew what was happening and why he was not responding to me as usual. I'm wondering if he felt ashamed or embarrassed. Does he know he got caught, or is he lost in memory lane? I couldn't help but notice his effort in trying to remember the lyrics of the songs, wondering if he understood the impact these lyrics had on our story. I began questioning if Marc Anthony was only ours or if these women shared that with him. Did they feel like I did when I heard one of those songs? Did it

112

connect them to moments with him, or was that only mine? The thought that we shared Marc Anthony made me feel robbed. I saw them as intruders, or was I the intruder? Everything was being lost little by little.

I did not know what to do. I did not know whether to leave him to Sandy, to these women who were visiting, or stay and wait.

Wait, wait--everything was waiting! Tired of waiting, I grew. I began to hate the word wait- my entire existence was reduced to this four-letter word. The wait seemed eternal, and I needed answers at once. Doubt was pinching my reality, making space in my subconscious.

Doubt as intrusive as its meaning encroaching in my world with my Science Project. I began questioning my loyalty to him and felt disappointed and furious. He lied - another lying bastard! Yes, they're all the same. In that same thought where doubt was my reigning king, I began disliking him. I hated everything that reminded me of him; sadly, the more I disliked him - the more I loved him, which drove me insane.

How could he lie to me? Why would he? There was no need. If he got tired, he could have told me, and I would have set him free. It would have pained me, but I would have understood. The pain he would cause would eventually go away, but after healing, I could still preserve good memories. I could have remembered him in a good light. But now, how could I remember him in a positive way? After healing, I will never forget he chose to lie to me. There would be nothing special about him. He now occupied the same category where others resided.

Love is a pestilence! I gave the head what belonged to the heart. I tried to convince myself that he was not the man I loved. It didn't work. Somewhere in that thin line where love and hate coincide, I could tune out the noise in the room, the women, and the family members and began focusing on the lyrics. *Love is All by Marc Anthony* is

113

playing, shifting the revolting thoughts into love. My head sank into my heart, and love was conquering me again.

Spirit sends messages in every form; messages are revealed to me through lyrics that answer a specific situation, and the message came loud and clear- I could no longer live in doubt. I must trust him.

I started evaluating myself: would I be okay if I left him to destiny? The answer was Yes, but my heart didn't want to chance him to destiny. As my eyes focused on his face again, my heart began thinking. I felt a calming sense; It was just him and me. I was okay. I felt okay. I just listened to the lyrics and sang along.

The mind is powerful; the need for approval, to justify everything, and to find miracles leads us to find answers in anything. To think that a song can be a clue to a life-altering decision is bizarre. What was bizarre was following through with it.

As the song finished, my attention is returned to reality, and emotions begin fluctuating again as I see Sandy across from me, his family staring at me with unsympathetic eyes. I wanted to leave, to run, and not have to be in the room with these people. I wanted to start over somewhere else. I couldn't deal with the vacillating emotions anymore, feeling as though everyone could see through my discomfort, facial expressions, or lack thereof, alerting everyone to my confusion and pain. I did not want to give them the satisfaction of watching me squirm and went home.

The following weekend, I visited him again. My anxiety peaked right before getting to his room, as I could never anticipate what kind of drama would ensue.

It became a ritual to sit on the planters in front of the rehab center to collect my thoughts and strength before going upstairs to see him. This time, as I watched couples go by, my mind wandered off to times I found strands of hair longer than mine in his car, but because it was the same color as mine, I didn't think much of it. After meeting Sandy, it made sense to whom the strands belonged. All the signs were there, and I chose to ignore them. I convinced myself I did not have enough evidence. Instead, I did not want sufficient evidence to incriminate him because having incriminating evidence would force me to leave him. I was not prepared to leave him.

He told me a few times that "he had given up a lot for me, but never what he sacrificed." I assumed it was his freedom. It was not his freedom he had given up; it was Sandy. It was those women.

Sandy made herself available to him throughout the years, endlessly waiting for him to return from whatever woman he'd left her for that season. Taking him back, always at his disposal, hoping he would eventually change. Perhaps knowing that real women grow tired of men like him, he would find himself again at her doorstep.

I always wondered if to women this level of forgiveness and patience is unconditional love or plain idiocy? The ability to forgive time and time and time again for the same wrongdoing is only known to mothers. I pondered if his returning to her after being with other women made her feel indispensable to him.

It perplexed me why he did laundry in his old neighborhood; there was a Laundromat around the corner from where he lived. Yet, every other Friday, he would drive to his old neighborhood at midnight to do laundry. I never saw the connection, but now, it made sense; it was all about her, their time together; the laundry was their meeting place, their hiding place. This was his proof that he was still available to her. I became jealous at this thought because, as clichéd as it sounds, there is an ethereal and romantic quality about doing laundry. It represents the end of a cycle of filth and the beginning of a new and clean one. A renewal of sorts, a clean slate.

It dawned on me that I had been so entranced in all the trauma and drama of the previous months that I had not thought about the possibility that Sandy was not a figment of my imagination. That I could not disqualify her. She was real. She existed, and she existed like the others did.

I felt filthy, like I needed to spin myself in the washer machine and cleanse myself of what I thought I had lived with him. As these images filled my head, I wanted to forget every time he touched me. Ironically, the same memories that connected me while he was in a coma for months were now the same memories assaulting me. Our memories helped me stay physically, spiritually, and emotionally connected to him; now, I could care less for them. I rejected them.

I felt how women feel when going through a divorce, getting rid of every item, picture, and wedding souvenir. I wanted all these images of us making love out of my head and my life. The way he grabbed my neck as he pulled me closer and closer to him when we were making love. I wanted to forget his kisses that made me weak to my knees.

To think that my quixotic ideologies about love put me in this situation. A kiss, a stupid first kiss that, yes, perfect as it was, was just a kiss. I should have left it at that. I didn't because he kissed me and transferred his essence to me. His tongue delighted my lips with an explosion of flavors and colors. His tongue asked for permission to come into my tunnel. He was paying his toll fee to cross the bridge, and as he entered- he injected his venom into my mouth. His venom caused a physical and emotional imbalance as his saliva traversed my organs and senses. He did not rush; he was not intrusive either. His kiss was inviting, fusing me to him. His tongue played in conjunction with his hands as he made his way to the back of my head and grabbed my hair. He grabbed it the way a confident man does, making my body feel safe, that I was secure in his arms, and all my worries could end.

The thought that Sandy and I shared him simultaneously aghast me. Oh! My stomach manifested its disgust in front of that rehabilitation center. How dare he, I thought. I started to sob; I cried the way one cries when one realizes something you love is gone forever.

My memory was triggered by the impending conversation my Science Project was to have with Sandy upon his return from our trip. Was he planning on dumping me if things didn't work out during the trip? Oh, the sheer cojones of this man! Was the trip the ultimate test of our relationship? What kind of man tells another woman that getting back together depends on whether a trip works to his advantage? Did he not care for her feelings? I couldn't help but feel sorry for her, for her pain.

The many months of crying desperately for him to come back to me. There, always there for him, in his world where very few ideas came at the same time, in a world of not remembering, I was there. Present in every moment, faithful, not letting go. Doing all I could in the spiritual realm to bring him back from the depths of infinity. The realization that he had lied to me was soul-crushing. The image I built of him came crumbling down like the Berlin Wall. I got played (who's the Science Project now?) His sob stories about how women mistreated him, hurt him, destroyed him, how they cheated, and the way they lied. He was the martyr, and the whole time - he was the liar. The one that had done those things to those women, the cheater, the destructor. He inflicted pain on everyone who came across him, injecting all his venom through his kisses and empty promises. Sometimes, the perpetrator projects himself as the victim.

Thoughts of him making love to Sandy the same way he made love to me made me realize that he was not mine, that he never was, that it was all an illusion; our existence was a figment of my imagination.

Enraged as I was, a part of me wanted to give him the benefit of the doubt. I found myself making the same excuses I have reproached from many friends before, "He's a man.

We hold men to such low standards! Women's process of forgiveness rests solely on the premise that "he's a man."

If I had a dollar for every time a cheating asshole got off on that line, I'd be rich! "He's a man" has become the defender of all crimes committed against women in the Court of Betrayals. The defending party must prove beyond a reasonable doubt that "he's a man" to get the cheating bastard exonerated.

A woman is betrayed by her lover and best friend; the best friend is thrown into exile by her friend for being a backstabbing bitch, while the man is exonerated on the premise that "He's a man."

A man abandons his pregnant wife for another woman, society accepts it, and when he finds the grass is not greener on the other side, he returns as if he didn't destroy that woman in the process. What is the woman told? She is told to swallow her pride and fight for her relationship because, at the end of the day, "he's a man."

A man does not return home on Friday and shows up Monday morning reeking of alcohol and sex; the woman, upset with every right to be, calls her mother to vent. Her mother's ingenious advice is, "Bueno mi hija, you must lie in your bed, anyway, todos lo hacen, "He's a man." Repulsive, I say.

I grew so sick of hearing that men can't be faithful, that cheating is instinctive to them. Hearing smart educated women saying, "Well, look at the divorce rate," as statistical proof to legitimize the argument. Yeah, look at the divorce rate, sky-high because women have begun to demand respect! We are not accepting boys as men, staying in toxic, abusive relationships for marriage's sake.

It was wrong. He knew it was wrong. That's why he just laid there, with all the shame. He knew that I held him to the same standards he held me. Had I failed, would he have understood? Would he have forgiven me despite his pain? Would he remember that it was a mistake? Just a moment of weakness, and that I loved him above all things. Would he have dealt with it? Nope, he wouldn't have, and if he did, it would be to make me pay back the suffering I caused him.

Men can't forget infidelities because it's humiliating to them to know that they were made a fool.

But for women, this humiliation is validation. All the suffering validates the grand, unselfish love we possess. To us, humiliation is this long-deserving suffering for being the descendants of the woman who ate a forbidden fruit. It's our payback, and we embrace it, hoping that our suffering gets acknowledged, and that mercy can be bestowed upon us, ultimately, reap a "good man" as compensation for the long suffering. Bullshit!

Find me a man who, after being heartbroken by betrayal or because his love does not desire him anymore, does not suffer. Men are not a different species from women. Their genetic composition does not code a cheating strand. No! They hurt the same way women do; they are taught not to. They have been conditioned not to be vulnerable and are emotionally desensitized.

Conditioning, nonetheless, is different from genetics. Men may differ in coping mechanisms- they drink. They drink until they become unconscious. They sleep with any broom willing to give them a night, any self-destructive activity that raises testosterone levels, and anything that proves their manhood, but pain is pain and is not gender biased.

We hold men to such low standards that we try to validate their cowardness and lack of integrity by comparing them to sample groups of rats and monkeys in studies. Why do we tolerate such lies? Why did I have to forgive or understand? I did not want to understand. I did right by him, which should have been enough to keep him faithful. I was his friend and everything else he wanted me to be. I walked many miles gracefully for him, without complaint, sucking it up. It was not okay for him to do that.

During my sanctimonious rant, Spirit murmured in my heart that "he and I got together while I was in a relationship with someone else (Dime el comienzo y te diré

119

el final)!" All my pious thoughts shifted, and at that moment, I accepted that this was karma collecting debt for my transgression. Moreover, how delusional were my thoughts since I was accusing a man who lost his memory!

I decided to go upstairs after that revelation. Sandy was with my lying Science Project. After a few uncomfortable minutes in the same room, I asked Sandy to speak. She agreed. I felt my heart racing as we headed downstairs. As we walked down the long corridor to the elevator, I could not help but notice how different she was from me. Her skin was not sun-kissed like mine. She had a beautiful face and long black hair and was shorter in height than me. Her speech was adorned by slang. I wondered how he communicated with her. She was different from the women who visited him. That may be the attraction.

I explained to her that it was as uncomfortable for me to be there and see her as it was for her. That I had no notion of her existence. Moreover, I was exhausted from all the drama and tension.

Surprisingly, she agreed to feeling the same way as I did. She told me that she had been dealing with his infidelities, the lying, and the back and forth for many years. In that same sentence, she clarified that they were no longer together (Are you kidding me! Why have you been harassing me all these months?) I had an Ally McBeal moment at that revelation, and I saw myself punching her in the throat as the words landed in my ear.

She told me she knew who I was because they were still going back and forth at the beginning of my relationship with the Science Project.
I asked her what she meant by "they were no longer together?" Sandy confessed to giving birth to her firstborn by the person she was living with. Allegedly, Lilly asked her to "stick around" hoping that learning about Sandy's existence would drive me away.

All the pieces finally clicked. Why didn't she fly out upon learning he had a car accident and nearly died? Why did she not visit the rehabilitation center as often as I did?

She had an entire family on her own. Human beings are capable of atrocious things in the name of "protection or love." The emotional pain and turmoil I endured during those months took me years to process.

I was in pure disbelief. Part of me thought she was making that up not to have to deal with his recovery, and this was a way of escaping without remorse. She expressed how "bad she felt for me because he played me." Because she was used to him doing these things to her, and in return, she also cheated on him, he would find out, leave her, and reconciled when the other messed up in whatever romantic situation they were involved in.

She began describing some of his behavior, and my brain could not reconcile that the man I was in love with was the same person she described. She said, "he would invite her to go places and leave her stranded." They planned to live together in the apartment he was living in when he and I met, leaving her homeless after moving in. He would show up with other women to places he knew she would frequent. He would stop calling her after meeting someone new and reach out when he was bored with the connection.

The information she provided clashed with everything I had come to know about him. This is the same man who looked for every opportunity to help others and possessed all the desire to make a difference in the world.

My years in the social services field told me there was pain behind what she was saying, manipulation even. There was bitterness in her tone. As she kept venting, I wanted to embrace her and comfort her. I did not. When people are hurt or feel threatened, they put up walls. I listened to her, and the more I listened, the more compassion I felt for her. It was clear that if she would subject herself to play out a lie for months, there was underlined pain.

She wanted to ignore that I was real, as real as she was to me. She kept ranting about "how good she had it," but I saw beyond her superficiality. I saw and connected to her pain; she was still upset that she did what everyone does for love: "Give it all, lose it all." In the same way, I gave my all to him, but loving him was a gift to me; clearly, this "situation" did not feel great, but I loved him and felt loved by him when we were together.

Her pain did not allow her to see the reality of this situation; she could not see that it was a human being laying in that bed– and not a penis. What puzzled me was why she felt compelled to share all that information if she was already in another relationship, with a family to raise, and had moved on? What concerned her about my decision to stay with him? Was she warning me, or was she being a spiteful woman, who, even after moving on, did not want him to love anyone else?

I realized that I could not leave him alone. I could not abandon him for the same reason because he was my friend; above all things, a human being who needed as much empathy and mercy. I loved him and felt I needed to see his healing journey through, even if we did not make it as romantic partners. I exhaled and started to tune her out as she continued with her disillusionment.

I looked at the sky and asked to be enlightened, and I remembered a quote from *Marianne Williamson's book A Return to Love, "When in fear, think Love is Real."*
The reality was that I could not change what happened. I could not change that Sandy existed, nor that he cheated, or if he still loved her. I could not magically "unlove him" because I felt betrayed.

I validated everything I felt; the love, the disgust, the fear, the hate, the need, and began operating as a friend. I understood that it was useless to invalidate her story or pain. I could not invalidate mine either. In my heart, I knew that he loved me every second I was with him. Better yet, I felt loved by him. We might never be together, but what I felt for him was enough to carry me through just on memories. I remembered how good he was to me, how he made me smile; he loved it when I burst into laughter as if his number one job was to make me happy. I remembered the last "I love you; I am so glad that you are mine, never change, I would never change a thing about you, I like being with you-with you it's never a dull moment," right before the accident. I thought about all these things and felt the importance of 'for better or worse.' Well, it does not get any worse than this.

This was the test.

When I returned from my daze, I explained that "she was free to do whatever she wanted. That I would stay around for whatever he needed. I would not abandon him, and I would deal with his lies when he could handle them."

From that point forward, I began operating as a friend and not a lover. I visited him regularly, as I did before the conversation with Sandy. I was there whenever he called, whether the call came in at one o'clock in the morning or three in the afternoon. I embraced it. I felt honored that it was me he was calling. I made sure that whatever he needed- I was there for him.

The process of recovering from a brain injury has many highs and lows as the patient is regaining strength and recovering memory, with many frustrating moments for the patient and those providing support alike.

It was becoming cumbrous to deal with him in his recovery. He was angry, and hated everything. I understood that his healing journey would be complicated, and to my advantage, his anger was not directed towards me. Seeing him bad-mouthing people who were helping and loved him was challenging. To hear him say "he wanted to die", or that he would "hurt himself." I was in a constant state fear and prayer.

His anger was merely frustration for not being able to do things for and by himself. He went through periods of depression, which was understandable. It was uncomfortable to hear him talk about himself that way, but the optimist in him always persevered. It was easy to not give up on him because he fought. Despite the depression and self-hatred, he pushed himself to go to therapy every day and as many times as he was requested to. He did extra sets of exercises to challenge himself. He went the extra mile to help his recovery, which was admirable.

Over those months, I grew emotionally and spiritually fatigued. Life had not stopped for me. I was still a mother, full-time employee, and student. I managed and always made him see the silver lining in everything. He would always comment on "how much he appreciated that I treated him like a normal human being instead of brain-dead." I never saw him as being "brain-dead." To me, he had lost his memory and ability to do things and needed help. It was sometimes frustrating to reason with him, but he would always get it.

Some of the most challenging times were when he began confusing events that happened with Sandy and me. To sit there as a friend, listening to him relate a story that involved the person that he cheated on me with, and not get sad. I would typically brush it off with an, "Oh, I do not remember that" or just smile, but gradually, that began percolating in me emotionally. I kept reminding myself that I was in the "friend's role." But I was still trapped in my body, and the "girlfriend" wanted to come out. She did eventually.

As time passed, he began recuperating rapidly, gaining agency over himself, no longer wheelchair bound, smiling more often, his vocabulary expanding ever more. While his recovery was promising, the antics, the never-ending drama with his siblings and some friends, kept deepening.

They did not understand how my Science Project could lose his memory yet remain protective of me. As if the more they hated me, the more he loved me. They accused me of getting in between his relationship with his siblings, which I did not. They accused me of having affairs, which I did not. His Stepmother had physically assaulted me by this point. One of his siblings was leaving death threats at my work voicemail. They tried everything to make him hate me, but it didn't work.

People try to destroy what they cannot understand. They did not know me. Granted, I understand the level of frustration and anger even when meeting me under those circumstances. Not knowing that he and I loved each other deeply. That we had history, even if unbeknownst to them. They chose to alienate me and see me as a threat instead of recognizing that despite all the humiliation they put me through, I stayed by his side. That should have been their confirmation that I was in it for the long haul. Instead, they chose hate. They chose to judge me without giving me a fair shot. They did not consider that he might have loved me. They did not consider that I was good for him. They wanted to destroy me, even if that meant- further destroying him in the process.

He was finally released from the rehabilitation center and had made such progress. He was not 100 himself, but he was on his way. His friends of many years helped care for him. He eventually started doing a lot more things by himself. We spoke numerous times daily, but I did not visit him at home. I did not trust his family or his friends. I found these people capable of anything, and I was tired of the confrontations and the threats over the phone. I was tired of feeling unsafe. We would only see each other if his older brother drove him my way.

It drove a wedge between us, but I was just tired by this point. It was cowardice, but exhaustion makes the path to surrender easier. Moreover, I had children to look after, and once the threats started coming in, I had to decide between love and my well-being.

It was more than emotional exhaustion; it was more than cowardice. I had suppressed my feelings, and when I began to process all that had transpired in those months, I was incensed and sad. I knew we were over. I lost him. I knew his family would never let us be happy, and he still did not have enough agency to tell everyone to 'fuck off' and let us live our lives.

I loved and wanted to be with him, but I had a hard time forgetting that the relationship I envisioned in my head had cracks in the foundation. I couldn't forget that he lied to me. Images of him being with other women became ingrained in my subconscious, and every time I spoke to him, I had these images of him with Sandy and the probability of others. I had to ask myself if I could forget the lies dealing with the constant harassment of some of his family and friends and all the demands I already had in my own life. The answer was a 'no' for me. The stressors of all those external dynamics were already weighing heavy on our ability to communicate effectively and to show up as partners.

We began arguing frequently because I did not want to wedge a bigger gap between him and his family by disclosing that his brother was making death threats and, therefore, did not feel safe visiting him. I did not want to explain that my hands were tied because his family would not accept us. The more I retreated, the more he demanded physical intimacy.

One random day in October, he called me, accusing me of being unfaithful, which had become the norm because people were in his ear, but this time, I snapped and replied, "And what if I was? Didn't you do the same?"

Usually, he would hang up and call back a few minutes later, realizing his behavior or anger was unwarranted, but this time, he didn't. I didn't call back either. I called him back the next day to clarify that I wasn't being unfaithful. A part of me wanted to get back at him but couldn't because I was still in love with him, but I was angry at him. Now, it was me who could not remember love or that we were worth fighting for.

I did not want to remember love. It hurt to do so. Life would see it that I never got to tell him that because his phone became disconnected. I assumed that he had temporarily unplugged it to sleep for a while; I called every day, wrote him letters, and sent him emails to no avail. I didn't hear from him for eight years after that. He disappeared from my life like all the men did without any explanation. He vanished the way my grandfather did, the way I moved around without any explanation. The same way my father was gone. He disappeared out of my earth's hemisphere as Enoch did.

For years, I researched newspaper obituaries looking for his name and rejoicing at not finding it. I wondered if we would still be together had the accident not happened. I wondered if he'd moved on- if he loved again. I wondered how many times we might have missed each other by seconds in the street of this giant New York City pavement. I wondered if he sensed me or if he remembered me. I missed him, and I remembered him every day - in everything I did and in everything I said. I cried sometimes.

Eight years passed, and his memory was ruminating in my soul, prompting me to call his number one more time. He picked up, and my heart sank at the sound of his voice. We spoke for hours like we usually did before the accident and even during his recovery. It was as if time did not elapse, except that it did. Life had taken place. I was in love once again, and he had married and divorced. From that marriage, he had a child. He got his kid, and I was elated for him.

Today we are good friends. We often speak about how cruel it was but remain grateful that we are still in each other's lives despite all the obstacles, the near-death experience, and the separation.

He taught me that men are not Science Projects. That love could never be relegated to such mundane and insidious arrogant endeavors as thinking that "we," any human being, can change or fix another. We must step into love knowing that risks are involved, yet the payout for those risks are enormous and fulfilling to the soul, whether the relationship lasts or not. Love does not come with an expiration date. Love will transform as needed, but love will always be love. That to love freely and abundantly is part of the soul's journey on earth.

He remembered me, and I remembered love.

I also remembered that:
In real life, not all love stories have a happily-ever-after ending.

The Game

In an instant, in one second,
two lives are changed forever in the blink of an eye.
Love is put to the test:
To be forsaken or to prevail is one of the tests that the
players of this game must overcome.

Time and destiny are the referees,
They're setting the rules,
the players have been selected (they're you and me)
The obstacles have been set, the game must begin...,
You are to forget me.
My touch must become unfamiliar to you.
My thoughts must not reach you.
for if one does, your love is immediately revived.
The challenge is for you to love in your unconscious state of
mind.

No flowers in our paths
Just thorns that penetrate the skin making this journey bleak.
No sun during the day
so, light may not be a guiding presence as you search for me.
No full moons,
since its face will point you towards me.
No rainbows, so that hope dies with thee.

Angels, angels want to intervene,
but they can't or the lesson won't be learned.
The lesson, what lesson? What is the lesson?
Is it strong enough?
Is it loud enough?
Will good prevail?
Will love conquer all?
Will I stay or go?
Will you go down memory lane, as unknown?
Is that the lesson? (I don't know)

Two soul mates found each other in their last life...,
They began to play the game,

129

He did not remember her.
She remembered everything.
He forgot love…
She reminded him…
And he remembered love.

For my Science Project

The Man in The Ice-Skating Rink
It's Complicated

Walking is the ultimate solution to a broken heart. I walked until I couldn't contain the pain, and the calluses on my feet developed. I was walking to mend a broken spirit. It's a dumb concept, but it helped me. I enjoy walking. It provides me time to think, debrief, be mad, resolve, ignore, and acknowledge how bad others have it.

I was in that stage where only walking could do something for me. I had no vice. I had no voice. I was existing to exist, just waiting for something magical to happen and renew my sense of pride, of strength.

I had reached the stagnation point in my life that all women face. The moment where complacency slowly creeps in and reigns until light comes in. The level of stagnation where we forget ideals and wonder if there's nothing left but to settle. We settle for what's comfortable, for what does not challenge us, and at its root, cheats us of our sanity and the right to achieve our highest potential; even cheating us out of the right to be loved.

I was comparing "love" to "quality of life," sometimes brought through loneliness or all the complexities that life will surely bring every one of us. I believe in "absolutes". As I kept walking and admiring the city streets, I reminded myself that there were absolutes. He taught me not to think in "absolutes." It is a concept, and it's not real. It can't be one or the other. Almost a decade into this relationship, I was hoping to teach him the opposite: That absolutes does exist. There's love and hate. There's darkness, and there's light. You want to, or you don't. There's simplicity and complexity. He did not believe in many things. I grew up believing that anything is possible. He hated fairy tales. I lived for them. He simplified things to the lowest degree. I complicated them. I continued walking until I understood the lesson to be learned. There's a lesson to be learned. There always is.

131

He's the kind of man women have had at least once in their lifetime- experiencing a mid-life crisis, separated, done raising children, and with plenty of experience to lure an innocent bystander into his web.

He was candid because he had nothing to lose. He was engaging, a walking encyclopedia, aesthetically pleasing to the eyes, and most important of all, with the confidence of a horse. The kind of man that alludes to no commitment, it is what it is man, and if you get caught up in the game--it is on your recognizance.

Instead of running at first sight of someone like this, women think, "Well, let's roll up our sleeves; this level of red flags, emotional detachment, and inconsistency sounds like a challenge." Another part-time job to help the poor souls in the world find their way home. Another project with no deadline, another "quick fix-me-up" to free our minds from looking within and start working on our soul.

The excitement a relationship like that brings kept me in the race. Unfortunately, women are in the business of changing people. The rush comes from knowing that you can help people heal and that in doing so, you are doing the Lord's work, a walking Earth Angel collecting your good deeds so when Armageddon comes, God looks at you kindly.

The Big Gala

I had been waiting for this night for months. The Who's Who of fashion designers, political figures, not-for-profit EDs, CEOs, and Corporate America would have been there. It was what most of my friends talked about for months: The dress, who we would meet, and, of course, looking forward to the "dos and don'ts" the following day.

The morning of the big night, I woke up with my infamous migraine, which does not go away with a bottle of aspirin. The thought that I could not attend the Gala since my migraines crippled me for days upset me because the night was promising and I had a fabulous dress (So what, I'm a little vain!) I was determined to have a great night. I took migraine medications, rested, and prayed for the inflammation to subside by the evening.

Hindsight is 20/20, so looking back, I now see how little attention I paid to the signs the universe was sending me. The migraine should have been my cue for: "Run girl, run until you can't no more." It should have told me this was the beginning of a long uphill battle with conformity or non.

I wore a crisscrossed with a diamond brooch brown mermaid dress. I wore my hair down, as usual, partitioned to the side to give some mystery to the face. I arrived late but was able to make a grand entrance. I put forth my "I'm a model" walk, looking straight ahead and seizing the crowd from my peripheral view. There was little to grasp- just a bunch of middle-aged men in black suits and boring ties. The men worth looking at were accompanied by the worst-dressed women in the entire city..., but hey, to each their own. Better them than me, I always say!

I sat at the table, absorbing the design of the place and its architectural structure. I get lost in beautiful architecture. I sat there just imagining the hours of labor-how the concept was born, what inspired that structure, and its design. The team's excitement around building the

133

project and the pride everyone must have felt once the project came to fruition.

Looking at architecture always provides insight into my personal life. I think of a new project, creating the blueprints, the execution, the stakeholders, the crew, and how long it will take. True to my Aquarius Moon and Venus, the thought of being involved in something new and innovative always brings a sense of fulfillment to me, especially around love.

The tables were dressed in white linen, napkins elegantly folded by a gold serviette ring holder. Beautiful candles with exotic flower centerpieces adorned each table, accentuating the stunning architecture. The brochures and programs of the day were placed on the seats. Most people I noticed put them on the floor, and very few read them.

I began introducing myself around the table to those I did not know and acknowledged those I did.

As I raised my eyes, there he was "the long-uphill battle" vowing his head and signaling that I caught his attention. I perceived him to be in his late forties or early fifties. He wore a black tuxedo and a scarf, giving him that old Hollywood appeal. Flawless skin, his skin and lips were rosy- just the way I like it. His hair- sexy salt and pepper hair that makes men look so much more appealing and exciting; giving the impression that they may have something important to say because *wisdom is their mistress*, and they want to share her with you.

I prefer older men, as I consider myself an old soul. I have always felt that I was born in the wrong era. I love old-school music (predating my parents). I focus on lyrics rather than beat. I love history, philosophy, and anything that helps me understand how people and the world function.

As a child, I often got in trouble because where I'm from, children do not mingle with adults. I would just sit among them, hoping not to be noticed and shooshed away. I found their stories captivating, the wisdom behind every word they shared, and how their thoughts evolved; their remembrance of life and the lessons learned fascinated me.

134

While most of my siblings and other children were playing amongst themselves, I could always be found where the elders were, listening, amazed, and remembering their stories, pretending that I was in them. Therefore, it is no mystery that I feel attracted to older men.

He seemed tall, although he was sitting, and very slim. I could not tell the color of his eyes from where I was sitting, but they appeared penetrating, as if they had their own vocabulary. It could just have been the dark circles under his eyes that offered this intense illusion. While dark circles under the eyes work for Benicio Del Toro, it ages most men.

I graciously smiled- not a full smile- but the kind that acknowledges his presence and motives, you know, the - I see you fishing - type of smile. Still too afraid and trying to be Mr. Frank Sinatra, he muttered how I was doing from his seat. I nodded, implying that I was okay, asking myself why I was entertaining him. This exchange continued for a few minutes until I felt uncomfortable and bored. I did not want to look in his direction, which was inevitable as he was seated right across from me. I could not escape him, even if I wanted to. It was flattering that he was devoting this time to getting me to acknowledge him.

The long speeches were over, and the live band began playing while people networked and congratulated the event coordinators for a spectacular event. The band was playing Compadre Juan when I got to the dance floor. There is a physiological urge to dance whenever Perico Ripiao plays- whether you are Dominican or not. The beat of the drums, the güira, and the accordion take over every part of your body. The potency behind the drums reverberates through every artery in the body, forcing you to stand up, even if you have no rhythm. The ebb and flow of the accordion shapeshift the dead into a living being. The güira envelops the body in this clashing wave of seductive rebelliousness. Making this musical genre one of the most infectious dances one can dance to.

Perico Ripiao is a traditional Dominican Folkloric Dance and a subgroup of the traditional Merengue, which has become mainstream in the Dominican Republic and abroad in the last few decades. It originated in the Cibao region of the country, deemed for lower class society, linking its roots to a brothel in the Santiago region. During his presidential campaign, Rafael Trujillo traveled the country playing his political slogans to Perico Ripiao, thus popularizing this genre nationally. Perico Ripiao is danced in a two-step count, with a fast pace and low intermissions; the bodies collide as each dancer gyrates their hips, as an invitation to the naughtier side of life without being able to consummate its intention (unless you're good at it).

Compadre Juan is one of my favorite folkloric Dominican songs. It brings up memories of my youth as a Dominican born and raised in the United States- finding the balance between tradition and assimilation is challenging for all immigrants. When we first arrive, the desire is to be accepted by the mainstream. We focus on learning the language and culture and fitting it in. To an extent, there is a rejection of who we are because fitting in is so important. Nonetheless, when teenagerhood comes, the question about who we are is brought to our awareness. That part tells us that something is missing in our identity, and we find that what is missing is being connected to our culture.

Although we spoke Spanish at home and danced our traditional music whenever we had family gatherings, joining Alianza Dominicana, Inc., helped me connect to my Dominican roots, culture, and folklore. The organization gave me and many Dominican youth the necessary tools to learn our history while adapting to American life.

I joined a group of colleagues who congregated around the dance floor, talking about the usual politics and the latest news in business around the area. Shortly after that, Mr. Casanova made his way to the conversation, seizing the opportunity to be introduced to me.

- Hello, my name is Frank. It's nice to meet you.

I engaged him for a few minutes, we spoke about our background, and I gave him my business card since he did not have his with him- (this should have been another clue; I mean, how do you come to a networking event without a business card? Unless you're hunting or instead want to give off the impression that you are not). I pretended to be interested in what he was saying to be polite. But he's a smooth operator and noticed that I was not interested. He left minutes after as I turned my attention to the group, but he insisted that I owed him a dance, Bachata, to be specific, to which I replied, "We will see."

Throughout the night, he sought after me in a way that was not overwhelming. We made small talk, and he would disappear again (in those few minutes, he set up the precedent for our entire story).

I was by the dessert table savoring all the delicious sweets when he came from behind.

"Breaking the diet, ha?

Yes, asshole, I like desserts should have been my reply, but I just smiled and said, "Nothing I can't burn off in the gym tomorrow!" Followed by the "You better back off Buddy, look."

It dawned on me that I had given him my business card. If he called, which I knew he would, he would call me at work, and I could excuse myself for being busy. Eventually, he would get the point that I was not interested.

Three-Day Rule

Oddly, the day after, I was expecting Frank to call. He did not. I thought, ok, he's playing the three-day rule game. He will call me in three days, I bet. He did not. He did not call for three weeks. One cold day in December, I received an email:
"Break bread or a few drinks to toast for the holidays"?

Is he old school or what? I thought, who uses "breaking bread" anymore?

My mind did not register that it was Frank as I read the email. I replied to his email the following day. I remember thinking he was very clever. He wanted to know if I was comfortable enough for dinner. Dinner is always more intimate and more personal. It tells him I want to get to know him and might even be interested. Had I accepted a drink, it would imply that I was only interested in having a good time.
I replied to the email with: "Who are you?"

He did not reply, instead, he called. Ironically enough, I was swamped and could not speak to him then. I asked to return his call. I did call back. I called because I was intrigued (I'm a Christmas baby, the holidays can be lonely, and I had not been courted by anyone in years—A girl's gotta get some attention!)
Within the first few sentences of the phone call, I was guffawing. I had to remind myself I was still at the office (beware of men who make you laugh, for indeed, the day will come when they make you weep.) We spoke for an hour or so, and I was captivated by his intellect, insight, and playful energy. My kryptonite!
He asked me out on a date. I hesitated a bit, only to say, "Yes." He arranged all the date details. I was unsure about meeting him, but I knew that, if nothing else, I would laugh my head off.

The big day came, and I had yet to receive confirmation from Frank. I called his office and emailed him, but I was still waiting; therefore, the date was officially canceled to me. I took my inability to reach him as a cosmic sign that we were not fated to meet (I tend to blame the Cosmos when I do not want to do something). I finished my workday and headed home to wrap myself in covers with a hot cup of chocolate de agua while reading a book.

At the root of it all was fear. It is safer to be home drinking a hot cup of chocolate than putting myself out on the dating scene. I was scared because I had been single for a few years since My Science Project. While I wanted a new start, I found dating exhausting. I find the prospect of falling in love exciting, but the process of finding it intimidates the Anacaona in me. The lack of sincerity, authenticity, and intentionality keeps me at bay, coupled with the sheer audacity of some men, makes dating daunting for me.

I sat in bed with my hot chocolate, regretting my childish behavior. Frank and I planned to meet at Blue Fin, and I should have gone without his confirmation, but as a Capricorn, I comforted myself by saying that "normal people confirm things, even if it is a personal affair," and for him not to confirm was a tell-tale sign, that he was not serious.

My phone rings.
"You chickened out, huh? "Said Frank
I said, "Hello Frank. Of course, not (I did). I left you messages with your secretary, and since I did not hear back from you, I thought you were okay with canceling."
He asked, "Will you leave this old man in the cold waiting for you? Take a cab. I'll be waiting for you."

I regretted picking up the phone, but now I felt pressured to go even if I did not want to. I felt obliged since he waited so long for me.

I arrived at the Blue Fin, and Frank greeted me outside. I wore fitted tuxedo pants, a white long-sleeve shirt with a red tie tucked into the pants, and four-inch black pumps. He wore a long wool tawny trench coat and a black scarf. I don't know if he had frozen to death due to the extreme cold weather, but he appeared older than I remembered. He also seemed taller. I like taller. He escorted me inside the restaurant and was courteous, removing my coat and scarf as he led me to the table.

To my surprise, the date became a party of three as one of his friends joined him for drinks, at the realization that I might have stood him up. It baffled me that he did not ask his friend to excuse himself after I arrived (red flag #3-can this man get anything right?), but I wasn't able to judge after my tardiness.

His friend dominated the conversation for the next hour as if I were on a date with his friend and not Frank. I sensed Frank felt uncomfortable and nervous (how cute, men his age still get awkward on first dates!). We glanced at each other occasionally, trying to dilute the discomfort during this date. As we gazed into each other's eyes, I noticed he had enchanting Larimar-Emerald color eyes that were both bright and dimmed. His eyes told what his introverted nature would not. I wondered if his eyes expressed light, anger, frustration, hope, or despair.

I asked if we could go elsewhere, hoping we could ditch the friend and have more time to get to know one another.
"Does Camaradas sound good to you?" asked.
"Well, yes." He said.

We left. His friend drove with us.

Meltdown In the Ice

On our way to Camaradas, we passed through Bryant Park. Frank asked if we should go ice skating instead. I said yes (thinking this man just wanted to test if I'm spontaneous. I'm wearing four-inch heels, Sir, of course not!) Ice-skating we went. I later realized it was the only way he could ditch his friend.

Ice skating is a great analogy for life. Even if you do not know how to, you must launch yourself forward. Despite the falls, getting up builds the strength to go through life confidently. The railings provide the support you find until we are comfortable, and holding on is no longer required.

We sat down for hot chocolate to warm ourselves:
I started, "Why is an intelligent, funny, and handsome man like you single? Are you single?" He responded, "yes! Well, I have been separated for a few years."
I thought to myself:
Of course, you are, and your wife is a mean old bitch who made your life impossible, right?). I let him tell his story. He claimed what most men claim when they are out on the hunt.
"I could not deal with the arguments anymore. I fell out of love. I love her, but I'm not in love with her anymore."
"Of course, you're not. You probably sucked the life out of her until there was nothing else to love, I thought to myself."
"Did you leave her and move out alone, or did you leave her for someone else?"
"Well, it's complicated, he sighed. Technically, I did not leave my wife; she locked me out."
"I do not understand."
He explained how his wife was solely responsible for him leaving their marriage. He said she changed the locks to the apartment after he did not return home at a decent time (4:00 a.m.).
He continued, "women fail to realize that there's always someone else willing to play host."

"UH! Does she know that you are not coming back?"
"Yes, she knows. I was planning to leave anyway, and her locking the door made it easier."
"Was this the first time she locked you out? It seems bizarre that she would do this."
"Well, no."
"Did she think you were out with another woman?"
"She always thought I was out with another woman!"
"Were you?"
"Sometimes."
"Where did you go after she locked you out?"
"To a friend's house."
"Female or male?"
"Female."
"Platonic friend or with benefits?"
"With benefits."

Frank was his name, and too damn frank for me!

I continued, "so, where is this woman? Is she the reason you did not call for three weeks"?
"Yes! I was confused when I met you. It was one of those roller-coaster relationships, very negative and draining".
The way you're draining me, I thought.
I retorted, "what happened? Why are you here? Why did you seek me"?
"I can tell you're a good woman."
"How can you make those assumptions when we just met?"
"Well, you're educated, intelligent, intriguing, and have a lovely ass, may I add."
I ignored the last remark.
I continued, "was she not educated?"
"No. There was a time when the women I dated were sort of bimbos, not up there intellectually."
"Oh! Is that because you're insecure and want to feel in control?"
"There may be some truth to that. Huh!"

This guy is insane! Mija, run for your life now. So, I stood. I was intrigued. He has a lot of fixing to do.

Frank shared a dating experiment where he sought to date forty women in three months.

"What were you looking for?"
"My soulmate."

Is this guy delusional, or what?

"Did you inform these women they were part of a research project?"
"I wouldn't tell them they were in an experiment, but I would let them know that I just wanted to make friends."
"Were there any criteria for being a subject?"
"There were none. We met and hung out."
"Did you sleep with all 40?"
"No. Some remained good friends."
"I would be called a whore if I conducted such an experiment."
"Yes, but I am a man, and society glorifies me for it. Society calls me a Don, and women have made it very simple for men like me to get away with some of this. You see, the Feminist movement started, and you wanted liberation and equality; in this equality, women felt that they wanted to date openly. Therefore, many women did not care that a man was married or in a serious relationship. They dated whoever they wanted with unattached fun. In turn, men realized they no longer needed to open doors or be financially dependable because equality means just that - we can both do it."

Before he finished the sentence, I visualized my hand swatting his etiolated skin, but I didn't.

"Do you believe this for real? Are you holding women's desire for equality as justification for reprehensible behavior, such as using women as subjects or control groups for stupid experiments? or not being financially responsible to your children and your families?"

"No, do not misconstrue my feelings and respect for women. Women raised me, strong women, may I add".

"If this is the case, how do you partake in such experiments using women to your benefit and pleasure? How is this representative of the respect you claim to have for your mother, grandmother, and all the exceptional women who raised you? Do you have children?"

"Yes, I have daughters."

"Oh! If a man experimented with your daughters, how would you feel?"

"Terrible."

"Is this how you repay the women who cared for you?"

"Don't misconstrue my words, nor use them to chastise me. No, I don't believe that the feminist movement is responsible for it. Women have the most challenging deal of all. Not only must you subject yourself through birth and exploiting your bodies, but you must also be the economist, the psychologist, the breadwinner, the mother, the father, and every other title that exists. But I know that society has placed you in this box, and unfortunately, you have, in a way, agreed to it. You still do."

"Do you glorify yourself? (You - egotistical, self-centered, self-absorbed asshole, I thought.)"

"No, I don't. I do not think of myself highly because I did this. The experiment was a way of accomplishing something I had been curious about for some time. Some of those women got hurt in the process. I did not feel good about that."

"What did you think would happen?"

"I don't know. I figured those women were busy. I was busy. I would see them occasionally, and that's it. I would be upfront with them; there were things I would not accept: women with small children and a commitment."

"I thought you were looking for your soulmate."

"Yes, that's what I thought I wanted. Know that you're not part of the experiment. I like you; I really, really like you."

"I know how much you like me", I thought.

144

A woman could live an eternity and never realize that *we are not that special.* We believe what the last victim experienced would never happen to us because we're smarter, funnier, or sexier. We think our vagina is always better than the previous woman. It never dawns on us that we are going to be that woman he will be talking about to the next prey.

I followed up, "so, what did you find?"
"That there are a lot of good women and only a few good men available."
"You are included, right?"
He stared at me long enough to make me feel uncomfortable.
"Are you still experimenting?"
"No"
"Why are you separated and not divorced after so many years?"
"It just never came up."
"Is that it, or are you using that as an excuse not to commit to anyone else?"
"It just has not happened. I wanted to do it some time ago, but my wife needed health insurance."
"Run that by me one more time. Does your wife not work?"
"Yes, she does. In fact, she makes more money than me. She can't afford health insurance; it is too expensive for her."
"I see! And beneficial to you, I bet! You don't have to do the day-to-day marriage thing, like helping with the children, cleaning the house, and arguing, but you still get to be a heroic partner by contributing this way, right?"
"You're smart".
Not smart enough, I'm here, am I not? I thought to myself.
"Have you thought about going back?"
"I've thought about it, but I was not happy."
"Was she happy?"
"I don't know."
"Why did you fall out of love?"

"Time. She stopped taking care of herself; she let herself go.
Women do this often; you get married, have children, and
think taking care of yourselves is over."
"Do you mean weight or getting dressed up?"
"Both."

You try pushing a nine-pound human being out of your
penis, taking care of a chauvinist, womanizing, egotistical,
vain pig like yourself, and see how much time and energy
you have left to care for yourself! I thought.

I must admit that I did agree with him to a certain
extent. The daily pressures of married life weigh heavily on
women. One of the chief complaints many of my male
friends' claim is that women let themselves go. Women
allow the pressures of motherhood and work to close their
eyes to the fact that men need stimulation and intimacy.
If women began demanding and delegating
responsibilities in the relationship, there would be more time
for self-care, social gatherings, and stimuli, which would
preserve relationships.
I felt it was vain of him to leave his wife, who bore
his children and dealt with him for so long because she
gained weight. I understood his sentiments well; however, I
am always baffled at the double standards concerning self-
care amongst the genders. I am sure that Frank was not the
man she met all those decades ago, not physically or
otherwise.
Women, at least most, never leave their husbands or
partners for superficial reasons. They leave because the
connection dies along the way. Many women end up with
men who are not their "type," be it physically, financially, or
spiritually because for many women the deciding factor is in
how that man made her feel. Feeling supported, loved, and
understood by him. Women look for men who make them
feel safe, men who are dependable, and who will grow with
them. If the man becomes another child, another burden, a
stumbling block to her growth, the relationship will not work
long-term.

I wondered what or for whom he left his wife for. Men only leave their homes when someone else is willing to welcome them in. Likely, twenty years his junior, skinny, and not much up there (but hey, pretty and perky).

I entertained the conversation some more.

"What did you do to ensure your wife did not let herself go?"

"Nothing. I was working. It was very routine, everything. We dined in the same restaurant every Saturday. We would have the same arguments every week. I was fed up. I was bored."

"Was walking out on your marriage the only solution? What about marriage counseling?"

"We tried. She wanted to blame everything on me. There were two of us. I was not the only one at fault. Overall, I was a good provider. I was not the worst husband. I did not always cheat. I loved her. She knocked my socks off the first time I laid eyes on her. I thought that I would always love her that way. Men are visual and believe their woman will remain young forever. We remember you as you were, not as you are. I loved her. I could have never fathomed that this would have happened. I was crazy about her. I loved her with all my being. It was not all my fault. I admit to wrongdoing. I admit to not doing the best I could all the time. I admit to giving up. But it was not my fault entirely. There were two of us. She did not respect me enough. She did not support my dreams. I was always there for her, helping her accomplish her dreams, but my dreams were never big enough to be admired or to help her accomplish. Men live for their dreams. You take away their dreams and dignity, and what do they have left? Nothing! I wanted to do so much, not for me, but for her, the family, and for us. My wife was my world. This is how I wanted to repay her for everything. I wanted to have a great life with her, with the children. It was not always bad. It was great! Yet, there was no medium. She had lost all her respect for me, and I couldn't respect her enough."

147

"Do you think she loved you"? I asked.

"She adored me, and that was the problem. Women need to learn that there is more to love than just having children."

"What is that more?" I asked him.

"It takes sacrifice. It takes shutting up even though you know you are right. It takes adventure. Trust. It became burdensome. We would argue for days, sometimes weeks."

"We went from having sex in the bedroom to fucking in the hallway. Not that kind of fucking- don't get excited! You know, the type of fucking that happens when you are mad at your partner, you see them in the hallway, and you say, "fuck you," and they reply, "No - Fuck You!""

"Even sex became unbearable. It is as if she was being forced to do it, as if she did not enjoy the things that drove her crazy before; she did not want to do anything old or exciting. She did not want to please me sexually."

"Can you see why at times she did not want to be intimate with you?"

"I don't."

"Think about it I said: if in the back of her mind she knows you are being unfaithful, she could, for one, be fearful that you no longer loved her or were satisfied by her; therefore, why try? Secondly, you could have gotten her sick."

"She rarely knew when I was cheating. In fact, our highest sexual peaks happened when I was cheating. We would do it every day, two to three times a day. We would do it until we were both sore. The time she did find out was because men are stupid. We leave dinner or gift receipts in our pockets, knowing that our wives do our laundry. We come home with the scent of soap from another woman. But she would never know for sure when I was sleeping around. I had actual relationships that lasted years while I was still married, and no one ever called the house or dared to disrespect her. I would not have tolerated it. They knew my home was sacred."

Yes, you should have told that to yourself, I thought to myself.

148

He continued, "I would ask her to do things, and she was always too damn tired. I was tired. Trust me, I wanted it to work. If I thought there was a way to remedy our situation, I would have done it, but there's nothing to salvage. I love her. She is the mother of my children. I spent a lifetime with her. I don't remember my teenage hood, my coming of age without her in it. She helped me grow. She is the only woman I have ever loved. But it was unbearable. I could not do it. I was having racing thoughts. I could not make myself unhappy anymore. I could not make my children unhappy anymore. I could not make her unhappy anymore. It was not fair".

"The woman you left your wife for, did she have any bearing on this unhappiness?"
"No, I had been unhappy for the last five years or more. But we are taught that real men don't leave. They stay, and they see their family through. I wanted to be different from my father. I wanted to be there for my wife and children to ensure that neither had to go through the pain I suffered because of not having my father around. I wanted to grow old with my wife. I wanted to see us sit on benches to reminisce. It became so burdensome. I stayed as long as I could. But I get chastised because I made a decision."

Wow! Talk about needing a session.

I asked, "the woman you left your wife for, what became of her? Why are you not together? Was she not everything you hoped for?"
"She cheated. Ironic, ha! Yes, but I did not cheat on her. I was faithful to her all the way."
"I call this divine justice! Did you think a woman who witnessed you leave your wife of twenty-plus years for someone twenty years your junior, who doesn't work or has any investment in you would be faithful? "Ladrón que roba a ladrón tiene cien años de perdón."
"I deserved it (yeah!) I wanted to change my ways. I wanted to try."

I always say, "Men are always ready to change their ways for the woman who loves them least."

"What stopped you"? I asked him.

He responded, "It was just too complicated. She had lots of baggage. I had lots of baggage. We were sexually compatible, and that is it. She became a project that needed too much time to see materialized."

Unlike women, men only take on projects that benefit them.

"I, like most men, cut and paste. We take projects and complete them in half the time required. A project like her - takes too much time. I did not have the energy, the time, or the desire to see it through."

"How long did you stay with her?"

"Roughly two years".

"Was it a committed relationship?"

"At the beginning, I was committed. After finding out about her cheating, I forgave her. I wanted to be with her. I tried to help her sort out her life. She's a sweet girl. She loves me. Then, she cheated again, and I couldn't do it. I could not forgive her again. I felt disgusted. Moreover, I could not handle her partying, choices, and lifestyle. I moved out. I would see her. I would feed her. I would try. I got bored. I left."

"So basically, you're a scum?"

"No, I'm a man who's gotten caught up. I just thought that I could get away with it, and I did."

I must admit that I was both revolted and fascinated by him. I respected the honesty. I knew I did not want to get romantically involved with him, but I wanted to keep him around. Find out more about him. I knew that getting involved with him intimately would be my downfall. I knew that men like him do not rehabilitate. Men like him are always on the hunt. There is never any profound connection. He was cunning enough to manipulate me into his zone without me realizing it. I knew that a hit like that would be fatal. If for nothing else, I wanted to keep him around for pure entertainment. He was hysterically entertaining and intelligent.

Growing Pains

Frank and I went out several more times. The more I got to know him, the more apparent it became that he had been using this macho persona to hide what was pain. Like many men who have stored their unresolved traumas, they masqueraded it as laughter, promiscuity, over-indulgence, or behind their work.

He disguised his pain in cynicism, sarcasm, retaliation, despondency, and cruelty. The victim becomes the abuser. The abuser validates his wrongdoing by claiming his victim status. By proving over and over that he is the victim. They manipulate any misconduct by making their victims understand how they got to that point. It's an art. It takes lots of cunning. Pain can present as confidence, assertiveness, masculinity, and many other forms. Frank was no different.

Like me, he had childhood, motherhood, and fatherhood wounds. The people who were supposed to protect him inflicted these wounds, making it challenging to heal this level of neglect. When neglect happens in the formative years because we remain in contact with the people who neglected and abused us, the trauma deepens as it becomes a constant reminder of what transpired, keeping those wounded cells activated.

The earlier the foundation is damaged, the greater the chances the structure will become skewed in its belief systems, in relating to others, and how one shows up in the world.

Childhood traumas dictate how vulnerable we will allow the self to become as adults, influencing how we love and protect. Healing is not a job for the meek of the heart. Unless the damage is repaired through love and support of loved ones, therapy, and spirituality, it is unlikely to get rid of that pain. Over the years, we can mask and repress our pain and traumas, but one day, all the issues resurface with explosive effects.

Our parents are our first introduction to the world. Most importantly, if we have trusting and loving parents or caretakers, we grow up trusting and loving people. Many men find it hard to acknowledge their wounds, let alone find healthy healing pathways. His parents damaged him. His closest relatives hurt him. The damage was irreparable. To welcome his future, he would have to undertake the biggest battle of his life- confronting his past. And I did not know how much I wanted to participate in it.

The more we interacted, the worse I felt for him. His childhood, like mine- was pilfered. In different ways but robbed either way. We grew up before our time. You go through life trying to understand why those events happened to you—trying to understand your behaviors as an adult, trying to reparent yourself. His pain activated mine as if we mirrored each other. I knew his pain and understood why he hid behind laughter and cried when no one watched. I understood why he isolated when feeling overwhelmed. These were the things that began connecting us on a deeper level.

Part of me wanted to free him because our bond was deepening. Trauma bonds look a lot like love. You see your story validated through that person because they, too, experienced your suffering. Trauma bonds are a healing challenge- we either heal, destroy the other, or both.

Before I knew it, I was in a committed trauma bond relationship.

I believed in absolutes.
He believed in nothing.

I knew it was about to get complicated.

The Big Night

How many undesirable and tragic events could be prevented if we stop being so cunning? One thing about Frank is that he was full of energy, spontaneous, and vibrant. There was this vigor about him, and the more we got to know each other, the easier it was to become enveloped in his energy. He warned me on the train ride home on our first date that "he was like a worm that slowly grows inside you."

His dynamism, intellect, and passion for life were like larvae penetrating my skin until he carved a space so profound in my life and heart that he was the only worm I needed by the time I realized his existence. The weeks were flying by, and we had not kissed or been intimate, but I was ready to go to the next phase with him.

Most of our outings ended up dancing; this night, we ended up at Arka Lounge, located on 191st and Broadway. I was on the dance floor, challenging his masculinity while he watched me from the bar. He signaled me to join him at the bar, and I obeyed like a straitlaced lady. He turned me around, and my pelvis began gyrating, creating friction between my lower back and his desires. He twirled me once again, this time facing him. He looked at me rabidly. I thought he was going for a kiss; instead, he kissed my neck. His tongue massaged my neck while his luscious lips pressed into my veins. He must have sensed my excitement because he began softly biting and releasing the jugular vein as if contesting my prudence. I left his side to join my friends on the dance floor to reclaim my composure as I was stimulated beyond measure. I feared leaving a trail of lewdness behind since my body temperature kept rising and my knees caving in as he kissed my neck.

He followed me to the dance floor, and in the middle of hundreds of people, we kissed for the first time as if no one was watching. We left Arka.

Frank walked me home and pretended not to know there would be a continuation of the bar scene. I liked that he was cunning as well. I invited him upstairs as I had decided that the time had come for some AARP-loving!

As an art connoisseur, he began admiring the artwork in my apartment, and we began discussing the pieces. I lit candles, turned off the living room lights, and poured him a drink; I played Private Dancer, suggesting through music that he would have a private viewing at my love lounge tonight. He kept getting close, and I kept backing away.

Despite all the sexual tension, we did not make love that night.

I woke up to the warmth of his body and got up to serve him coffee and toast. He pulled me in tight as he finished his toast. His finger began exploring my Bearded Clam without talking, looking at me intently as if asking for permission to serve him the entire meal.

I was ready and able, but he was not. Junior wasn't. He needed a therapeutic session before sex (what is a girl to do? I listened). He claimed, you know—Voodoo. Most men claim Voodoo if the organ does not respond. It's easier to blame Voodoo than to admit that there may be a problem. I thought, "Brother, the only voodoo you have are those green leprechauns in your head." There's a saying that God gave us one mouth and two ears, so we listen more than we talk. The active listening worked because we made love with little to no intermissions between Saturday morning and Sunday.

AARP was electrifying.

Dam Sex

Sex is a potent exchange of energy. When emotions are not regulated, it can be confused with love. "Like grows into love," all in all, is just sex. There's only a physical connection- no respect but "respect for the organ." It is not love but "love for the act." The need to have it can be fatal.

I knew that getting involved with Frank would destroy me, yet my flesh and mind craved him, and it was stronger than anything else I had yet experienced. Loneliness, the need for intimacy, and connection confused me about whether I liked him, loved him, or felt sexually connected to him. Our affinity for each other made it hard to distinguish whether we liked each other as human beings, lovers, friends, or life partners.

Our bodies responded to this lustful instinct when we were beside each other. It was obsessive. Frank became an unlimited fountain of pleasure for me. It felt amazing. The magic was that we knew we were out of each other's league. We were two planets with similar atmospheres and the collision of our bodies, mind, and soul- was a catastrophe with a calamitous aftermath.

For the first time in my life, I was in a connection where I felt I needed someone. I had never needed anyone before, financially, emotionally, or sexually. I didn't need Frank economically or otherwise, but I wanted to need him. I began looking for deficits that I did not have to have him around as if I forgot how to do life and could only navigate it through Frank's lenses. It burned to need him. I felt uncomfortable needing him but found comfort if he addressed my needs. I pulled away many times, trying to manage the co-dependency I was developing for him, but I could not stay away.

If Frank called, I was there.

156

Time Is Not Always the Answer

Time is a tricky concept- ambiguous at best. It leads us to believe that if we just hold on and surrender to the situation, it will resolve on its own.

We have become so complacent, entrusting our entire lives to leaving things to time. "Give it time," people say, 'time takes care of everything' others believe. We have given complete control of our ship, and our captain is Time. Does time always heal? Does time always take care of the situation?

My intuition told me not to trust him, but my heart told me he was a "good man." I wanted to give it "time" and let the process unfold organically because I wanted him. My intuition kept resisting him, while my flesh and mind were fascinated by him. Perhaps finding out too much about his past heightened my distrusting nature.

My brain and heart vacillated between the man I met at the ice-skating rink and the man I was getting to know during the courtship. The man in the Ice-skating rink was always present. His past flashed through my brain when we spent time together (the women, the experiments). We were not committed. I wasn't. I thought I wasn't, but when he asked for exclusivity, I said nothing - I was exclusive.

He did not want a commitment, nor did I. Yet, neither could understand why we were investing any real effort in us. We were comfortable because the sex was great; we had great chemistry, laughed, and intellectually stimulated each other. We were willing to argue every day so long as, at some point, we would make up. We ran whenever things became overwhelming, too committed, too involved, too exclusive. The runner-chaser dynamic would define the relationship.

I could not forget the man who sat before me at the ice-skating rink, but I did not want to be hypercritical. I tried to push the man in the Ice-skating rink to the back of my mind for the man I was getting to know. Disturbingly, I missed the man I met at the Skating rink that cold Friday night in December. Frank was honest-brutally honest, but not deceitful. He was pompous and confident. He undressed me without even touching me. But the man I was getting to know could not even look me in the eyes, he was like a lost boy trapped in a man's body. He was full of fears, more than me, frankly speaking. His abandonment issues, sorrow, indecisiveness, compulsiveness, obsessiveness, and unhappiness triggered my shadows. The shadows I had worked nearly all my life to overcome.

Yet, I was falling for this version of him, the wounded boy, the insecure man. I felt as if I were being unfaithful! I was falling in love with two completely different men sharing the same body.

It got too complicated.

Frank legally belonged to someone else. For most people, it would not be an issue. It became an issue for me because now we were dating, making it one of the moral contentions throughout the relationship. It raised many questions for me (all of which I asked on our first date); for instance, what was it that he was gaining out of staying married? Was he seeking reconciliation? Or was he waiting for her to come back? Was he using this as an excuse not to commit to me or anyone else beyond a relationship?

A part of me did not want him to get divorced, as I was hoping he went back and worked things out with her, partly because he did not know how to close chapters. I was willing and prepared to lose him if he realized he was still in love with her. I hoped that if he did go back, he would realize that he was not, finally able to close that chapter and fully begin a new one with me. I wanted him to make that decision.

I did not know her. Even though Frank never spoke ill of his wife but expressed the relationship from his point of view, all he told me about her could have been a lie. She could be an exceptional woman. I'm a woman. I know the dreams and values instilled in little girls who become women. You belong to one man only. You stay, fight, wait for change, sacrifice, and love until it gives you cancer.

Divorce is different for men and women, and the benefits are different. The woman continues to carry on with the responsibility of the home and the children, while the man moves on to create more responsibility for someone else.

Men get older and date younger. Women lose their greatest years waiting for change and their husbands to return.

I began internalizing his inability to close chapters. While he claimed to be emotionally unattached to his wife, I felt like I was the reason he was not working things out with his wife. I feared the, "I have decided to return to my wife" call. I feared getting involved with someone like that because the ending is always predictable. I did not want to be part of that novela.

At my core, I knew it was fear that he would never marry me and never choose me as his last partner. This heightened my insecurities and abandonment issues. His indecision to close this chapter in his life to start one with me laid the awareness that I was falling in love with a man who could not provide emotional safety for me. The worst was betraying myself, as I did not want to do anything about it, hoping my love would change that.

I gave it time because he wasn't with her. He was not living with her. He would not see her unless it was a holiday (it was an excuse not to leave him).

The relationship unfolded in a way where my present-future life with him constantly competed with his past. He would be incommunicado from his children and wife, to resurface around the holidays to uphold the familial traditions. He would not have to do the day-to-day marriage dealings, but he'd show up on holidays, and everyone pretended to be a happy family. I would point out how disturbing this pattern seemed to me and how selfish it was for him to only be present during these times, and he'd reprimand me for it because I saw right through him.

For many years, this was his family; this is what they did. I understood this. He's a man of stature. He likes titles, and men with his background live for this. He still needed to belong to something to make up for his upbringing, for his lack of love.

While not having to fulfill the duties of marriage, he belonged to someone else on paper. He was normal in the eyes of society. At work, the Human Resources office will note in his paycheck the deductions that refer to him belonging to someone and, more importantly, that he contributes to the great institution of marriage. He's a man. He got married once. He's a one-woman man. He commits only to one woman, although he committed only on paper throughout his marriage. He lived for titles, for status. He still belonged to a group of people. He wasn't particularly interested in being financially stable; he was, however, very interested in belonging to something.

I understood that holidays were the closest he got to reliving his "phantom family" fantasy. I could always picture how the holiday scene would go; He sat across from his wife, referencing the patriarch and matriarch duet, while his children sat one across from the other. They would laugh even though everyone was uncomfortable. They knew Daddy had left Mommy. They knew that something was different; it had been different for years, but they laughed because it was Christmas, a joyous time. They laughed and exchanged gifts because it was Easter and traditions were to be kept. What kind of example is being set for the children if you don't pass traditions along? Father's Day came around, and everyone reminded him what an exemplary man he had been, even though he left and had not been back in years. And he doesn't call, and they don't get together unless it's a holiday, a birthday, or an emergency. This dynamic was the least complicated thing he had ever done. He's a simple man. He simplifies everything.

I understood his need to pretend, to belong, to even yearn for the family he had, and technically, they will always be his family, but I was in the picture now, and he claimed he wanted a future with me. I had to remind him that he decided to leave her, and while he did have financial and emotional obligations to her and their children, he was not obligated to spend every holiday with her. Had he chosen to remain single, then fine, I could understand him continuing this tradition. However, the minute he got serious with someone else, it was not acceptable.

It was never about excluding her, but certain holidays did not belong to her and did not exclusively belong to him anymore. Had he included me or blended our families, it would have been easier to process and accept these traditions, but he always told me that his children and his wife would never acknowledge me. He didn't introduce me to one of his children until six and a half years into the relationship. I am unsure if he said his children and wife would not "acknowledge me" to hurt me or keep me at bay.

Ironically, when I did meet one of his daughters, we formed an immediate bond, as if we had been friends all our lives. I spent the better part of our relationship as the phantom girlfriend his family knew of and knew to call whenever he went missing.

He would go to dinner to discuss family matters with his wife, and I watched him getting dressed up in his finest clothes to meet with her. When we went to dinner, he looked like the homeless person from around the corner. But it was to prove to her that he was doing well, while I knew he wasn't.

I wasn't jealous that he was still "close" to his wife. I believe that if you ever loved someone you can remain friends with them. And no, not for superficial reasons, or because you are hoping to rekindle the relationship but because this person was important to you at one point. You claimed to "love" them. The relationship didn't survive, but love can always transform. So, the issue was not that he and his wife were "close", but it felt like the life he was building with me shamed him somehow.

I never pushed anything. I would just point out the obvious to me and allow him to process the information and decide in time.

I trusted time too much. I forgot that time is not always a problem solver. I forgot that time is the thing that makes things very complicated.

"I Love You, You're Perfect,
Now Change"

Passive-aggressive communication was the norm in our relationship, and I was as much a culprit as he was. We loved the theater, the scenery, the stage, the ambiance, and being able to discuss the show afterward over dinner.

My birthday gift was to take him to the hottest Off-Broadway show, "*I Love You, You're Perfect, Now Change.*" The musical explored the quandaries of dating and the distressing myths and truths behind dating, falling in love, and the future.

Taking him to the play was my subtle way of telling him something needed to give. I thought what a great way to get a conversation going and explain that if he didn't change, we were over for good. Like most plans meticulously calculated, it backfired. It was the "Aha" moment as I realized- it was me who needed to change.

The show revealed to me all the areas I needed to change. Many aspects of our relationship were full of indecision, impulsivity, possessiveness, and manipulation. The relationship oscillated between cold and hot and bewildering. It revealed that for several years, I did not know if I was dating the aloof, narcissistic man I met with at the ice-skating rink or the one I had come to know throughout the years.

The man in the Ice-Skating Rink cared nothing about closing chapters. Women from his past were in our present, leaving messages, hoping to reconnect with him. Frank did not know how to cut ties; he would not call back (to my knowledge). But he never learned to tie loose ends. Women are better at this than men. Women will go back and close chapters while men leave them open in case they need to revisit them. He did not know how to say, "I'm with someone else now; you can't call me, is not right." He had poor role models growing up.

163

The show forced me to think deeply about where we stood in our relationship. We were not committed. I couldn't say that it bothered me until I realized I had been compromising on my non-negotiables until the show.

We were exclusive but not committed. Frank gave me exclusivity (we only date each other) in exchange, so long as I knew we weren't a couple. He never officially said we were not a couple, and I never asked for clarity. His behavior was an unwritten contract that we were not.

The times he considered us a couple was because he felt insecure and threatened about the things he made me experience, such as previous lovers circling back around under the pretense of friendship, the not closing chapters, and the not tying loose ends hurt him. He understood in those instances what he made me feel. Some people lack introspection, a moral compass, an emotional regulator that signals, *'Hey, your actions have hurt someone deeply.'* Some people only learn when they experience the same pain they inflict on others. I never intentionally created those situations, but when they arose, I did nothing to stop them. I felt justified. It was passive-aggressive and small of me.

The man in the Ice-Skating Rink was always present; he would go on hiatus from time to time to allow Frank to peer through for a while, but even in those 'absent' moments, he was 'present.' He was the silent partner in a business where he controlled every move, but no one saw him during the company's meetings. He reaped the benefits of his investment, the bonuses, and the profits that being a silent partner brings.

He was the director of our movie, meticulously directing every step and how the scenes unfolded, but when the film premiered, the only mention of him would be during the credits.

The show brought me back to a disturbing night while hanging out in a local bar in his neighborhood.

A beautiful black woman greets him, "hello Frank"!

164

He responded, "hi Lana, how are you? Lana, this is Leydis".
I said, "it's great to meet you, Lana".
Lana scanned me from head to toe. I instinctively knew she was not pleased to meet me and was about to ruffle some of my feathers. Unbeknownst to me, Lana was the woman Frank left his wife for, who happened to live upstairs from the bar we were at. She was viscerally upset.

Lana returned to her seat. I asked Frank who she was to him, and he confirmed. I asked for us to leave. I could not believe this man would take me to a bar where his ex-girlfriend would frequent and who lived upstairs from the bar.

Lana followed us to his house and began frantically ringing the doorbell. When he didn't answer the door, she called his number repeatedly. Frank shared that unless he answered, she would just go on a binge.

I gave in and told him to let her in. I have this stupid ability to connect to people's pain and feel responsible for it. I did not want Lana to binge. She entered the apartment and sat on the couch next to me. Her energy felt vexing; therefore, I quickly moved to sit across from her. Frank sat on the same couch opposite Lana as no other seats were available. She lit a cigarette.

Lana was youthful, slender, and full of life, yet something in her had dimmed. I wondered if Frank dimmed her. I felt compassion for her. I could tell she was still very much in love with him.

I began thinking about how much women love that we sacrifice our dignity for love. I asked myself if I would ever allow myself to stoop this low. I quickly reminded myself that I had already traded my dignity for love when I stood with him despite knowing he was still legally married; by allowing this woman to come in, by tolerating the calls in the middle of the night and tolerating these undefined sequences of events in our relationship.

She began speaking about their relationship, what he had done to her, what she had done to him. With every sentence, her body moved closer to Frank's until she was beside him.

I sat across from them as Psychologists do in a session with their patients. Just analyzing them, how they responded to each other, how they looked at each other, and if the feeling was mutual.

Frank was uncomfortable, red-faced, and started flaring his nostrils the way he always did when feeling upset, being caught, or irritated.

Lana's hands found their way to his leg until they reached his crotch. He removed her hand, and she did it again. He did nothing. I silently watched in sheer consternation. I wanted to see how much farther he would let her go (if it could go any farther than this).

She warned me that Frank would leave me, to go back to her. She warned me that he had done it many times before. He obsesses over someone only to stop the calls abruptly. That he would disappear; when this happens, I should know that he has returned to her because Frank belonged to her. I thought of Sandy and how she had warned me about my Science Project.

Lana claimed they had an inside joke for me, which confused and appalled me. She knew I was the girl he was dating from Uptown. She knew I had children; therefore, he must have talked about me with her. My Science Project came to mind.

According to Lana, he only yearned for her breast, for her body, for her vagina. She claimed that his Junior only responded to her. Right after making love to me, he always had to go back to her so that she could finish the job. Although I knew it was a lie because he had been mine for so long now, and he did not need anything to be aroused by me. My presence excited him; nevertheless, the comment bruised my ego, although I knew it was a lie.

I asked Frank if he loved Lana. He said, "No, I care for her. I wish her well. I now know and understand that we cannot be friends." Lana claimed he was lying. She warned me that he was saying that because I was there. Her tone began to change. His frigidity hurt her. She began swearing. I told her "That I do not fight for men, nor do I lose my composure. He's an adult allowed to make whatever decisions best suits him." I sat there disappointed with myself, upset at him for not respecting me, not respecting himself, but "girls will always be girls." Women always think that our pussy is better. That our vagina has the magic serum that would mend broken men. That our vagina is so good it could get a drug addict sober, a thief into an honest person, and a liar to be truthful. We think that our pussy heals countries (may start wars - but never peace). I, too, was guilty of the *"Pussy Redeemer"* complex. The Pussy Fixer. I thought so highly of my vagina I nicknamed her "La Caridad del Cobre" for all the miracles (assholes I fixed) I performed. Go right ahead and say it out loud: This woman is demented and delusional!

Until then, the empathic being in me would have allowed her to stay the night, but her comments irritated my ego. I was not her enemy, and there was no need for such low blows. I wanted to show her that I was in command. I commanded him to ask her to leave (at the risk of her binging), and he complied.

She warned me as she exited that "he's a piece of shit. Soon I will be experiencing the same thing. That I will remember her when my time was up."

I stood up. We came to my house and had vengeful sex.

The man in the skating rink was always present.

Always.

167

Love Is Patient or Not

My relationship with Frank was a slew of opposing forces that worked together; we were both peace and war, purpose and rudderless, spring and winter. We were a trampoline of raw, beautiful, and suffocating emotions. When we were good, everything was excellent! We viewed life the same way. We were affectionate, dedicated, and willing to fight for each other. We shared similar desires to see the economic-political status of our community change and worked together on many personal and professional projects.

There was so much of who we were that bonded and bounded us. We had a similar upbringing, faced many adversities, and overcame it. The chemistry between us was both beautiful and destructive. Yet, we did not invest in us enough. Our good times, as well as sex, kept me in this relationship. In these times, I saw our potential as a couple. When we were good, we behaved as a power couple and a force to be reckoned with.

The problem with falling in love with "potential" is that we often dismiss the reality of the situation for quixotic fixes or expectations that it can be better. We ignore the toxicity, pain, and disrespect for the possibility that, if we try harder and give more, it has all the ingredients to make it work.

Our bad times were just like our good times - extreme. It felt awful when bad times came around (these were often, more towards the end). It was like going through a crack addiction withdrawal. It got us sick to our stomach, irritating our very existence. Our tolerance went out the window as if facing a stranger or a foe. That was the thing about us; we never understood that we were not fighting each other but the issue at hand. We were not the enemy- our problems were. There was a magical love between us that became overshadowed by the lack of effective communication, the deafening silence, the indifference, and the need to up the other were the real enemy. Not us.

It was an emotionally charged and toxic relationship. We became friends only to become enemies. We confided in the other only to use it as ammunition to chastise the other. We deeply cared for each other, yet there was this barrier that neither of us could overcome. As if the entire universe conspiring against us was not enough, we conspired against ourselves with our deeds!

So much of our relationship was about letting the other go. I reminded myself that love is relatively easy and simplistic. You either like somebody or don't. You want to be with somebody or don't. I was confused because he often spoke about how much he cared for me. How I had been the most serious relationship he had after his wife. But, for some reason, his words and actions were not in accord. I surmise that I did not want to acknowledge that this was what he told all his lovers, that they were "special too." "They were the most serious relationship he had been in since his wife." We always think our vagina is better.

There was a lot of competition between us. A constant need to outsmart the other, outplay the other. Who liked the other the most? Who could annoy the other the most? Who was willing to relinquish the other faster? Who could sabotage the relationship more? Who gave the most? Who hurt the most?

We both acknowledged that it was an intolerable situation but neither felt strong enough to call it for what it was. We settled. Perhaps, we didn't settle, and we were just incapable of honoring each other as we were…, imperfect.

Partly because we had both failed, we failed in previous attempts to have normalcy in relationships. Perchance, the sense of failure stemmed from thinking that this was the one relationship to prove that he and I were as normal as any other couple.

We knew we wanted to be in each other's lives; what was hard to figure out was - in what capacity. We were too emotionally involved and with much resentment to have a platonic relationship. We were too sexually attracted to each other not to have sex in the equation, and I was not going to be his booty call. It seemed that individually and as a couple, we had too much baggage to make our relationship work. I believed in absolutes, and he believed in nothing.

The relationship missed the mark on the three pillars that make a relationship thrive- trust, respect, and safety. Our love was intense, but not the kind of love you want to keep around. Not the kind that nourishes, that empowers, that is healthy. It was not fairytale enough, or at all. It was the kind that manipulates and wants to hurt. We showed up for each other in all the wrong ways because we were not listening to the needs of the other. We both compensated for what the other lacked, yet the halfway meeting point was not stable long enough to get us through. The entire relationship was a weekly break up or argument, yet we could not be apart for more than a week. It was terrible if we were together, and worse when we were apart—at least that was the case for me.
We wanted it all. We wanted to be emotionally attached but not committed. We tried to break up but remain friends without the foundation that makes friendships work. We wanted to have the other at each other's disposal. We were brutally honest with each other but did not want to hear the truth. It was hard for us to be completely vulnerable with each other because we did not feel emotionally safe with each other.
He did not seek me. Well, he did, but not emotionally. I sought him because I wanted a partner I could confide in, but he was a transactional partner. He fixed everything with money, and I wanted him to understand that I was not for sale and that his transactional love language was not what I needed. He would shut down, and I interpreted it as him rejecting me. When I would shut down, he felt I was punishing him.
Frank and I shared many of the same wounds, but I had been working on healing my wounds for many years. Frank's wounds manifested in a way that was not beneficial for him, for me, or our relationship; and he failed to

recognize that he needed to heal them. I knew that men with his level of neglect and abandonment issues always leave. They do not know how to tie loose ends and do not need closure. I lived with the uncomfortable feeling that he would leave me any moment, so I would break up with him as a preemptive strategy not to feel abandoned (again). He hid behind his protective wall to permit him to walk in and out as he pleased. People like me conceal emotions. We act as if we are always in control, but underneath it all, I am frantically padding away like a Duck.

I, too, sabotaged the relationship in every way possible. I, too, was bitter. Too resentful. Years of micro-aggressive comments- how he shut me out and made decisions that impacted us deeply without consulting me, made me resent him. But I acted in control, or I thought I did. I wanted to protect him, and for him to feel safe with me. Frank was almost twenty years my senior, but at times, I related to him as my child, as I am sure he regarded me as a child as well. I felt responsible for his well-being. I tried to do everything I could to make him happy, but it was not enough. His issues were beyond me. Our happy moments became far fewer in between as the years passed. I wanted to run, and for the first time, I did not.

Despite the dysfunction, we stood together and bought a home four years into the relationship in the hopes that we could continue fighting for our love. We tried to be as normal of a couple as possible. We made beautiful memories with my children in that home. We celebrated many milestones, some of which were happy, sad, and distressful moments in our home. But it was home.

When I decided to be with Frank, I felt that this relationship would be different for me, and I hoped it would have a different outcome than my previous relationships. Here was a man who had already experienced life, dated, and was accomplished professionally. I did not have to fear that he needed anything outside of what I had to offer him (foolishly, I thought). I assumed he knew what he wanted because he was older. I liked the fact that he was older. Plus, he did not want any more children (great plus). I didn't have to worry about explaining that I did not want any more children or if this would be a contention point in the relationship. But this backfired on me. I forgot about the man who sat before me and told me of his experiments, how he left his wife for another.

I became enveloped in him, in his insight, in our sexual intimacy. I'm not sure how much of it was ego and how much was compatibility. When we spoke, I heard compatibility, which I wanted to hear. Often, I would catch myself saying, "I'm going to have the last word."

We failed at seizing the moment. We failed at being happy. We failed to allow ourselves to be happy because we were both guilty of feeling "guilty." Guilty about walking out in previous relationships, not fighting for love, for what matters, for a section of earth where we can have our time frozen, where surrender rules. For not fighting for a piece of our Eden. Guilt precedes fear, and fear is paralyzing and forceful. So, we settled. We settled for good sex, for having someone we could call "ours," ultimately, because we were tired of waiting for the real thing.

Complacency is why people who do not love each other stay together. People stay in relationships and marriages out of comfort. Comfort allows us not to have to restart, not seek that which the heart truly yearns for. Comfort allowed us to sit in what we know and have learned to manage over time. Comfort does not require reinventing the wheel. We settled.

Our relationship was intoxicatingly comfortable. We had each other when we needed it and walked out when we wanted.

He was so confused and hurt that, at times, I did not even know how he would make it through the week. I felt consumed by the relationship, and so did he.

He vacuumed the energy and youth out of me as I sucked up all his mid-life crisis, being left only with the residual dirt from his mess. Part of me did not even mind, so long as he felt okay. I failed to realize that the more I vacuumed his issues, the more I recycled filth into my dust canister, thus amplifying the stress and depression in my own life.

I resented him for knowingly deploying me to his Ground Zero and not providing me with a mask to protect myself, and not providing the proper equipment to prevent me from getting sick. I resented him for disrupting my routine and the situation; I was mostly indignant at myself for allowing myself to stoop so low. Where were my values? My morals? It was easier to blame him than to admit that I resented ME.

He never asked me to take on anything. To me, staying was earning another stay. Another fight in the name of love, a martyrdom trophy for my *unsolicited benevolence*.

I became more demoralized, debased, and faithless each year I spent with him. The simplicity of his presence completely altered my faith. I, who always believed, believed no more. I did not believe in God. I transferred all my frustrations and resentment onto God, but Frank grew spiritually. I was mad. I blamed God for my depression- for not protecting me from someone like him. I became detached from my divinity, and the less I spoke to God, the worse I felt.

I kept sinking lower and lower, and I thought this was normal—I embraced it. I, who always believed, no longer wanted to. I allowed myself to feel this pain for the first time in my life.

Eight and half years later, he felt better as I plunged into a universal black hole of pain, only to know that in a few months, I had prepared and released him of all his demons. Frank had cured himself and was about to make his final exit.

Mission accomplished as women are in the business of fixing people!

He resented me for disrupting his routine, his life, and his psychotic ways of relating to life, people, and emotions. He resented me for pointing out that he had issues. Before meeting me, he did not deal; he did not feel compelled to close chapters. He resented me because for the first time, he understood that not closing chapters is irresponsible. It's as reckless as having an STD and not telling your sexual partners. It is as irresponsible as breaking up with someone by telephone or email.

His issues triggered my abandonment issues, my body drama issues, and my issues about the possibility that I may end up alone. The latter became the more real for me and the one I feared the most. This relationship failing was proof in the pudding that I sucked at relationships. It meant that every meaningful relationship and every investment I have made went down the drain. I felt like a failure as a woman. I failed.

I had put all my eggs in his basket because I had no other choice. There weren't other baskets where I could have placed my hopes, dreams, and personal goals. Frank's basket was poorly woven, and the hemp was not strong enough to hold space for what I brought. The basket began dismantling as I placed each of my eggs in it. My eggs crashed – in the same way buildings implode as each egg hit the ground.

In retrospect, there were other baskets, but I was tired and demoralized. To begin the journey with someone else was a task I did not want to undertake. The words he spoke unto me over the years left me feeling like I would never find love. And I did not know or want to "unlove him."

I tried to leave him. I did not know how or where to get the strength to do so. The inability to leave him depressed me even further.

The Best Vacation Ever!
The Journey to Unloving Me

The room went dark, as dark as when I was a child, except that now I was in my thirties, panicking in the corner of my apartment. The room was spinning. I did not know where I was, although I knew I was home. The sense of hopelessness was hugging my body tightly like a soothing hug. The more I tried to breathe through the anxiety, the tighter its grip on me became. I was crying the same way I did when I was holding onto my mother's leg, begging her not to leave.

I knew I was in trouble.

The voice in my head kept screaming that I was 'useless.' I damaged everything I touched (I heard it in my father's voice..., ahi vienes tu a joderlo to'), and that I should cease to exist and not burden anyone else with my useless existence. The voice became obstreperously commanding. "Just do it. Do it. Kill yourself," the voice commanded.

My head was pounding. My foggy vision brought my awareness to a bottle of Malbec and an Advil bottle on my nightstand. "Take every one of those pills and end this suffering you cause yourself and others." The voice got louder and mocked me as if the voice was an entity with more agency than me.

I began praying, but the voice was louder and interrupted my prayer. The pit of my stomach was saying, "No, don't do it, just breathe," but the voice was forceful and kept pressing down on my desire to live in the same way my uncle used to press down on my leg as he molested me. I felt powerless and paralyzed in my own body and mind. The walls started caving in on me. I saw them getting closer and squeezing me out of existence. I gave in. I followed the voice and took as many pills as possible with a sip of wine until they were gone.

I quickly realized I had made a colossal mistake after finishing the bottle. I tried vomiting, but it was too late. I was getting very dizzy. My stomach and head manifested its disdain for what I had done to them. I was now panicking, barely crawling into the living room. I phoned my girlfriend La Cubana and told her what I did. She came with her pregnant self and husband and drove me to the hospital.

"What a shame," said the EMT as he brought me into the hospital on a stretcher, "Such a pretty girl." All I remember saying was "Sorry." All I've done in my life is apologize. Sorry for existing. For being such a coward. Sorry for not doing things correctly. Sorry for not being strong enough. Sorry for being such a bitch!

The hospital transferred to a Psychiatric facility in Westchester, NY, after a few days of being admitted. I was so embarrassed to be in there - that I let my desperation get me into yet another mess. More embarrassing was being processed at Security by a former Alianza peer whose words of encouragement were, "Diantre Leydis, te dejaste coger. ¡Que pena!"

I sat in that lobby and saw people I considered to have real mental health issues (more than mine, or so I thought), and here I was, taking space from someone who needed to be there. I was sorry for that too.

For most of my life, I have felt I was depriving someone of their rightful space by my sheer existence. I never allowed myself the room to validate my pain or any trauma because someone else always had it worse than me. I lived my entire life invalidating how I felt or how traumatizing most of it had been. I would not allow myself permission to cry because I always had to be the strong shoulder for someone else. I couldn't weep for myself because I was ashamed of being so sensitive.

My sensitivity has been one of the contentious points between God and me. Why make me so sensitive if this was going to be my life? Why not make me strong to be able to deal with life? My exterior was tough, but since I was a child, I grappled with feeling emotions, events, mine or others deeply. It takes me longer to process what I am feeling, why I was feeling any way, and what I have do to address it because I must understand it from every angle.

I was ashamed of being smart. Being considered pretty brought me anxiety because nothing good ever came of it. I hid. I hid my talents, my brightness, my spiritual prowess. I hid my sensitivity.

That's the thing about trauma: *the accretion of trauma, the years of microaggressions against my physical, emotional, and spiritual being, took a toll on me. Every word and action slowly crept into my soul and attempted to erase my divine blueprint.*

I was tired, so I hid. But I hid in the loudest ways and got away because I felt no one was listening. I hid and just wanted to go home. Not my physical home on earth, but to that place that has been calling me since I was a little girl.

No one would ever think that bright, "everything-is-well," "laughing-out-loud Leydis" ever felt darkness. Perhaps because I am not the prototype of what sadness looks like. My sadness is not wrapped in torn fabric alerting the public that I may be sad. My biological father always told me "When sadness invades you, shine your shoes." The light in my eyes have never physically lost its glimmer. The luminosity of my smile has never floated in murky waters..., at least never in public.

So no, I have never worn my depression or the dark energy that has been following me since I was a child because I try to find the silver lining in everything. I have felt duality and polarity, light and darkness ferociously pursue me. It's probably the only force that has always courted me. I have felt the presence of God in my life and the Devil closely following my steps. For every lead God gave me, an opposing force threw everything at me, hoping I would succumb to it.

Since childhood, I had these recurring dreams of a man dressed all black following me. I could never see his face, but his presence terrified me in the dream. I always woke up from the nightmare right before the dark entity could grab me. I think we get so tired of being tired that the things that scare us the most, we're willing to face them and not deal with them ever again. I was tired of that recurring dream and the anxiety it provoked in me days after.

In one of those dreams, I said while dreaming, "I am not waking up. I am going to see who this Cuco is." I saw his face, and it wasn't a face at all; it was just darkness, a void, like going through a tunnel with eyes wide shut. It was just a scary and formless energy; it felt evil. It tried to grab me, and we got (the Devil and Me) into a fight. True to my High School nickname - Tyson, I beat the crap out of him. I understood the psychology of dreams and was most likely fighting my shadow, my darkness, the trauma, and abused I endured. It was probably the fear that has paralyzed me, the men that have debased me, all the "Cuco's" who have put their hands on me. I probably fought ME.

The three weeks I spent in the Psychiatric Hospital left me with some valuable life lessons. I met some exceptional people. Highly functional, caring, loving, intelligent individuals drugged to non-existence. A blank stare in eyes that held all the stars and knowledge of the world.

All the days are the same there: Alarm goes off, fix the bed, shower, eat breakfast, get medication, attend one-on-one interviews with the doctor, and then attend mandatory meetings where coping mechanisms and other topics are discussed. Then, there is lunch, visiting hours, dinner, and more medication.

I kept to myself mostly, but the guys always conversed with me. There was Mike- an artist diagnosed with bipolar disorder. Mike knew every museum and artistic period in history.

White Tommy- a person with schizophrenia, was versed in everything hip-hop. Then, there was Sunshine, diagnosed with every possible mental health disorder in the DM5 book. He was the oldest in the group but also the funniest and brightest mind ever. Talking to Sunshine felt like conversing with someone who has existed throughout human history!

Nicole was my roommate. A stunning Black girl diagnosed with schizophrenia who loved wearing beautiful and colorful headwraps. She barely spoke, but when she did, it was profound. Her voice was soothing. She called me Lady D. and would salute me by reminding me to "get out of my head." "It's all I've done since I was five," I would tell her. She always reminded me that "I wasn't five anymore". It embarrassed me that she knew that I was always in my head. More embarrassing was that she perceived that I hadn't realized that I had grown up or that I was still that little girl afraid of everything and everyone.

I didn't allow visitors, mainly out of shame. *I have worn my 'shame' and 'guilt' as the finest of silk. As if that shame and guilt provided me a softness that soothed the discomfort of what it actually felt like..., needles pricking my skin, which is what shame and guilt feel like. Yes, I hid behind the comfort of my shame, and all the guilt I have ever felt because it convinced me to do and go through my darkness alone. After all, my poor choices led me to that moment.*

I was embarrassed that people would see me as not in control or in my best position to project that everything was fine. That I still had the bull by its horns.

Nothing was fine,
          and
              I could not hide it anymore.

Those three weeks allowed me to think about everything I had endured in a more calculated way. It made me realize that all the years of therapy, all the self-help books, all the versions of the bible I read, and all the people I had poured myself into trying to heal them and make up for my pain had done little to nothing to heal me. But darn it, it was the first time in a long time someone was caring for me.

I sat with the abortions, and with the lies I accepted and told myself. The disappointments I had faced, the trauma I had lived over and over. More impacting was the realization that, except for being molested, I participated in everything that had happened to me through my choices.

I got involved with men seeking love while never looking at myself lovingly. I was never merciful with the parts of me that were unhealed. The parts of me that fought against every single obstacle presented my way.

I never held my father responsible for not keeping his end of the bargain, and therefore, every love story ended like him- ABSENT! A never-ending loop of impermanent relationships, like all the men I attracted.

I had to acknowledge that up until that point, I had been absent from my own life, in and out of my own life, emotionally speaking. I blamed men for negating the love I initially sought from my father and, more atrociously, denied myself.

I failed my intuition at every phase of my life, as if daring life itself. I accepted the fact that my lack of boundaries gave reign to everyone to treat me as a doormat because I treated myself as a doormat.

I had to answer all these questions:
What was love? What did love look like to me and feel like to me? Who could give me the love I sought if I never met a man who could match what I desired in a partner? What did I desire in a future partner?
I had to answer myself for allowing sadness to sneak into my mornings. The way the sun's rays snuck into my bedroom, gently gleaming into my eyes, letting me know the night was

over and a brand-new day awaited. Except that instead of sunshine, my repressed pain turned my bright mornings into prolonged dark and cloudy days. I had no brand-new days. It was Groundhog Day every day.

For the first time, I saw myself implicated in my unhappiness. I understood that I couldn't continue to drag my father, my mother, the toxicity from my childhood, and the relationships I brought to my life because of my lack of awareness around "who I was."

It was a painful realization because no one was to blame but me. While I didn't have a choice around my childhood experiences, I had a choice in how I showed up for myself. I was responsible for honoring the parts that needed tending to. I was accountable for a happiness that was not attached to anything or anyone else other than me despite my trauma.

But that is what trauma does, it silences you bit by bit. You become your trauma, the only lens that makes you whole, although a fragmented view. Your trauma gets louder as your spirit shatters with every traumatic event or experience. You begin to think that the experiences that come into your life are what you deserve, whether toxic relationships, staying in virulent work environments and spaces, or around people that are vexing to the soul.

Sadly, this wasn't my first suicidal attempt. The first attempt was when I was nine; I found money in the bathroom hamper. I thought it was a miracle! The next day, I went to Hobbyland and purchased crayons and pencils for my fourth-grade classmates (I have always been altruistic, Dominican Robin Hood).

When my fourth-grade teacher asked where I got the money to buy everyone in class a set of crayons, she phoned my mother to verify. I forgot to tell her I didn't tell my mother I found that money. Money was constantly oozing out of the hamper or throughout the apartment. I knew I was going to get a beating. A big beating for taking things that did not belong to me (I remember thinking, I wish someone were this upset when people took something away from me, like my innocence).

I was so frightened that when I got home from school that day, in my despair, the only thing that came to mind was to end my life (I was tired of the beatings). I went to the kitchen, took a knife, quickly headed to my bedroom, and locked the door. While pointing the knife to my stomach, I began asking God for forgiveness. An inner voice told me "NO!" like it did this time. I was sobbing. I heard a knock on the door and quickly hid the knife. I did not get hit that day.

I would attempt it again as a teen when I ingested hairspray (I slept for what seemed a day). I don't think anyone noticed. No one ever knew what pain I carried. I was just a loud, rambunctious, precocious, and rebellious child. That was my fault because I was always smiling. I was trying to be heard. I wanted someone to listen to my pain through my laughter. To be honest, I didn't even understand my own pain. I failed. Perhaps the loudness was to muffle out the pain. I read books, wrote in my journal, and got as loud as possible. I was always fine. Life was always great.

I was popular (perhaps for the wrong reasons) but felt uncomfortable in large social groups. I could always sense when I was the topic of conversation by the stares that were half-moon smiles and full-moons filled with disdain (even if they thought I wasn't looking) and the double-handed comments. I have always been intelligent, funny, a protector, and resourceful, and somehow, people have always wanted to keep me around for those reasons. I never cared much for social groups or to fit in.

I was obnoxious. Obnoxious but reliable. Everyone could always count on me. I relied on myself and God. It was difficult for me to divulge or be completely vulnerable because I was so ashamed of my story, especially the things that I allowed because of my past.

Somehow, my inability to tell my story to others developed my spirituality. It grew in my loneliness. I pretended that all was well, but when nighttime fell, in my moments of seclusion, I always went to God to weep, even as a child. Perhaps not having a face in front of me as I shared my story, or the day's events made it easier to rely on God. I didn't feel judged; I either felt a nudge after speaking to God that sprung me into action, or I felt complete peace by talking to God. Yes, God, my books, and my journal were my best friends for a long time.

I knew to go to God when my uncle molested me. I knew to pray even though I didn't know who taught me. I knew there had to be a force more significant than the circumstances I was facing, and it listened to me because I did not feel that I had that on earth. I have claimed God even while being beaten, raped, or having a great time.

This suicide attempt felt different. I believed God was disappointed with me. I was upset at my myself for I did not take the proper steps to care for my mental health. I allowed the impositions of the world get me to a place of no return.

I sat in those mandatory group meetings at the Psych Ward thinking, how little I thought of myself. How much disrespect I had allowed in my life. I thought of my friends rushing to my house to rescue me in the middle of the night. The recklessness of it all, and possibly leaving my children motherless. How unkind I had been to myself my entire life. Indeed, I faced significant traumas and unfortunate events, but despite my traumatic past, I managed to forge ahead.

It dawned on me that I never celebrated myself and did not think I was worth celebrating. I remembered all the dates of tragic events, but except for my children's births, I can't remember any noteworthy milestones I have accomplished. I think I have made it almost impossible for people to celebrate me because being the center of attention feels uncomfortable, yet not a single person would ever think that of me, as I can also be an extrovert when needed.

I sat in those mandatory meetings, taking stock of the fact that despite my origins, I managed to remain a good-natured and faithful person above all the atrocities I had faced. I obtained a college degree despite my High School Counselor's lack of faith in my ability to graduate High School (The Capricorn in me loves proving me wrong). I managed to raise my children despite the financial and emotional deficits I had faced.

For the first time, I began looking at my story as purposeful because my entire life signaled that. I understood then, how skewed my perception of myself was. It was groundbreaking. I had it with the lockdown and wanted out. I had to prove to the Psychiatrist that I was ready and able to join the world before being discharged.
The thing about voluntary admission to the Psych Ward is that - the discharge is not so voluntary.
It baffled me that I wasn't diagnosed with any mental health disorders because my whole life, I have auto-diagnosed myself with at least five of them.
I was recharged and had enough time to think of the years ahead and that this three-week vacation was a much-needed break!

I also thought:
I need to start taking better vacations.

I was discharged the day before Thanksgiving. I sent a text on the family chat stating that I would host dinner. I got home from "my vacation," went food shopping, and began preparing for the Thanksgiving feast as if nothing happened; very much the way I have powered through everything in life as if nothing happened. I needed to do something normal, and nothing felt more normal than serving people. I prepared that meal, knowing that everything in me had changed.

Another version of me died in that ward; however, for the first time, I was proud that a version of me passed on. It was the first time I had a choice in my death and rebirth.

Coming out of that vacation, I understood that nothing else could ever be the same and that I must take myself seriously. The only person who can affect me to such a degree is me, and I would no longer accept behavior towards me that was pugnacious to my soul or being.

I would no longer allow myself to disrespect my intuition, boundaries, or self-worth for anyone or anything. More importantly, I would never attempt against my own life.

I finally understood that despite the car crashes, all the near-death experiences, and the trauma I have faced in my life, I survived them all for a purpose. My life's purpose haunted my mind, like a muse haunts a poet, and love is always after the heart. I didn't quite know my purpose or what I was to do with that purpose other than to serve others; inherently, I knew it was bigger than service.

Shortly after coming out of the mental institution, the relationship with Frank fully deteriorated, and there was no return. We were both exhausted with our love story. Frank left, and after more than eight years and a love story that left me not knowing who I was anymore, I was at peace with him leaving. I told him there was no getting back together.

I left that relationship decimated in every way possible (emotionally, financially, spiritually, and physically). I was still madly in love with him. Nevertheless, this time,

a

little more

(in love) with me.

Pages Flying in The Wind

I handed you my book,
An anthology with all my experiences
to help inform you, and, having read my biography,
You and I collectively create a new compendium.

Untimely is your lament.
The story has come to an end,
I wrote the last page…
And we do not make it unscathed.

The words have withered away,
The ink has completely run out,
The verses that professed my love to you
Did not reach your merciless heart.

I gave you my book autographed inside,
With the ink of a past that in your pen
could have been signed with smiles.
In the certainty of the Present,
we could have titled so many trilogies!
In the hope for tomorrow...
complete our story with rhymes.

But you forgot to read it!
The dust has ruined the pages.
The corollary of your abandonment
has left my book discolored.

All that is left from that story.
are acrimonious words narrating a tale.
Perhaps futilely recited.
Perchance, poorly constructed,
Maybe, perhaps, it was a vision!

Fragments of a vivid imagination,

Your character now an entelechy-
that categorizes me as lyrics,
in your book of elegies.
Pages flying in the wind.
Words amassing an irreverent
and humiliating solitude.
A forgotten love in literary shelves,
A lamentation for not being able to change the end of this
tale.

To the Man in The Ice-Skating Rink
(My Greatest Teacher)

Today, Frank and I are great friends. Many years later, after the healing was done, and we were able to humanize the other, we were able to fully forgive one another for the pain we consciously or unconsciously caused. We forgave each other for not being able to show up in a more loving, empathic, compassionate way in our relationship.

There are so many things I am grateful to Frank for. I am so grateful he is still a father figure to my children. I am grateful for the growth the relationship brought to me. Despite the breakup, Frank and I continue to support each other in life.

The romance, and need for each other dissipated over the years, but a beautiful friendship withstood the test of time.

Frank taught me about patience and mirrored back to me the love I needed to give to myself. That's what those under the sign of Aries do. They teach you about the "self."

Frank was like a volcano in the mountain that has been my life. The lava (dysfunction, passion, obsession, and love) burned my land, but after the dust settled (catapulting deeper inner healing) the soil became fertile. Fruitful. Detached. Unapologetically free.

If not for this experience with Frank, I would have never dug into the soil that is my life. I wouldn't have explored the roots in my tree to see why the branches (failed relationships) were weak. I had not yet experienced a romantic relationship that I felt was healthy. Was it those men? Was it me? Or was it a problem in my lineage?

Frank left me with an encyclopedia of knowledge about life, about the way I love, about what I wanted or was no longer allowing in my life. And I am forever grateful for that.

After the breakup, I remained single and, more importantly, abstinent. The thought of another man touching me appalled me. I wanted to restore my relationship with myself without the interference of love, a relationship, or a man. It was

189

important to address all the stacked-up trauma (sexual, emotional, and all the AL's) I had endured.

It would take five years to process my relationship with The Man in the Ice-Skating Rink, but it wasn't Frank. In fact, it wasn't any of the men I had been in relationships with; at the end, they were "projects," a means to not deal with the fact that I had been a coward all my life. Merely a frightened little girl who thrived on sacrificial acts, a never-ending loop of toxic relationships to justify the fact that I failed to work on the most important task handed to me at birth—MYSELF! That was the most important project I needed to bring to fruition.

I had to face the fact that at the center of all those failed relationships, be it with men, my parents, friends, or society; I was the common denominator in all those failures.

All the years in therapy, self-help, and self-development books I read, seeking God and a connection to him, were not the only preparation required to complete or reshape me as a "project."

I had to unlearn all the programming around love, and the distrust I had in men. I had to reparent all the versions of me; the three-year-old who felt abandoned. The five-year-old me who was molested, the teenager who felt misunderstood, the eighteen-year-old single parent powering through life, and the thirty-year-old me who allowed herself to be debased by a man who did not love himself.

Let's be clear,
                    I didn't either.

I Almost Let Her Die

I almost let her die,
I forgot that she needed tending to,
I was too busy tending to the ongoing struggles of life,
Integrating all the lessons learned so as not to fall again,
while she was disintegrating from the inside.

I almost let her die,
Her soul withered away with every lie.
Conditioned to water everybody's garden while the flowers
in hers
- died.

I almost let her die,
She multiplied her five loaves of bread to feed everyone else,
yet neglected to feed herself.
Constantly praying for the blessings of her family and
friends,
but felt ashamed to ask God to send her blessings as well.

I almost let her die,
Her vision was impaired by tears that did not belong to her,
The pressure in her womb pained her with every step
from carrying so much weight, pain, and the swords that
stabbed her lumber spine.

I almost let her die,
and I am ashamed of that.

One day, I said enough!
It's time to pour back into your cup.
I dressed her with the foliage of fall,
I retreated her inwards to realign with her soul.
I sat her by the Hudson River to cry out to her ancestors and
ask:
Where were they?
When were they going to intervene or help?

Healing her wounds became my Ten Commandments.
I built her a home that only she can reside in,
I decorated it with all the glorious hopes, dreams, and
aspirations she once held, and gave her new ones to rebuild
her shell.

I opened her eyes to the beauty that lay within her,
I opened her mouth to utter incantations that would change
her future and would heal past and future generations.
I sat her by grace and bathed her in oleander-infused water,
I reminded her that she, too - mattered.

It took some convincing, patience, and time.
Today, she sings alongside swans,
The flowers in her garden are blooming again,
Her walk makes the celestial court beam with pride,
Her eyes are clear and fulfilled.
I see her today, and I'm so proud of her...

For
She chose to live,
And not die

How I Started Fixing the Shit

I considered myself to be highly intuitive, yet, in every unfortunate event I experienced, I went against my own knowing and intuition. There were times in my life when I felt as though my intuition failed me. I had to recognize that it was I who failed my intuition.

That is what trauma does- *it makes you believe you cannot trust yourself.* The inner dialogue, intuitive nudges, or messages you hear are invalidated because after the initial awareness (message) you receive, ten other messages come through that are misleading. I began testing myself as training to trust myself more.

I began reading about metaphysics in my early twenties as I was exploring my spirituality outside of religious denominations. Metaphysics explores reality and existence, and as I questioned what my purpose was, I got interested in Astronomy which explores the universe. I was looking to understand my journey from all levels (spiritually, intellectually, and psychologically). At this point in my journey, it was important to find ways to protect myself energetically as I continued to help myself and others in an honorable way.

My work in healthcare introduced me to Emergency Preparedness (EP) which teaches the steps to follow before and after an emergency or natural disaster happens. I began viewing my intuition through the EP steps to protect myself.

Through Emergency Preparedness there's a concept called Situational Awareness which is the knowledge an individual experiences at any given moment. Ultimately, situational awareness decreases exposure to danger and the potential for human error.

I view Intuition as Situational Awareness. God, the universe sends me signals in low and sometimes loud signs to heighten my awareness, be it physical, emotional, or spiritual awareness. The more in tune I become with my own body, energy, and thought pattern, the easier it is for me to remain alert to potentially noxious outcomes. The purpose of this type of monitoring is not to live in fear, but to remain alert to avoid danger.

Situational awareness follows three models: Perceiving Processing and Predicting.

Perceiving (something is off)
How often have I perceived an imbalanced energy? A suspicion of sorts, and decided to go against it? Be that I had a thought (go left but went right,) or a dream I remembered in the morning with a message. The numbers, messages on trucks, a conversation, or a song I heard that brought awareness to me. Those signs often feel like goosebumps, an eerie feeling in the pit of my stomach, and sometimes a sharp pain in my body as the message is trying to come through. Sometimes I can't fully understand what that "something off" is about, nevertheless, the nudge is for the purpose of exploring what it could possibly be. There are times, I may not fully understand at all what the nudge is, but the nudge is persistent, which is calling for me to act. That action can be as simple as leaving a place, a person, or a thing.

Processing (what is off)
I have always felt connected to everything. I find cues and messages in almost everything. An alarm goes off as I think of something, I take that as a confirmation. Asking God a question and being presented with the answer through a song I have not heard in years.
Perhaps, is listening to the voice of a beloved who departed. What does the dream mean? Processing the intuitive nudges, feelings, and signs you get is the decoding of information that is being received.
For example, If I feel sadness when things are seemingly going well for me, or I know that I woke up in a happy and joyful state, I ask myself: Why Am I feeling sad all the sudden? Did I watch something that made me feel sad? Is this sadness mine, or Am I intuiting someone's energy? Did I

hear a song that saddened me? Did I think of someone or a place as I heard it?

As I started checking in with me, I began regulating my nervous system. Trauma stays stacked up in the body. After I was raped, the years that followed, I would wake up with severe pain in my body, usually a couple of days prior to the date it occurred. Those were the same pains I felt when it happened. Emotionally I had done the work. But the body remembers trauma. Once I started noticing the patterns about the trauma surfacing back up, I began doing mindful activities to release the symptoms that would bubble up. For example, I intentionally stretch my body days leading to it. Or I would go dancing. I would write a poem about "loving me." Today, I no longer need to do this practice. But in the first few years I did.

The same thing happened when I had those car accidents, one which left me paralyzed for a several weeks. The body remembers. The physical abuse I endured, left with me with similar trauma, when people make certain gestures that make me feel unsafe or a threat to my physical body. I may flinch.

Traumas dysregulate your system. The way you breathe. The way you interact with others. It is important to be mindful and intentional about breathing. Keeping the body active to release negative toxins. It is also very important to intentionally bring in joyful moments into your life. That could be through laughter. Music. Sharing moments in nature.

This is why processing "what is off" whether that's physically, emotionally, spiritually is important to healing.

Predicting (what is the outcome if I don't listen to my intuition).
There is an adage, "Spirit walks before man". My higher self has already seen or experienced the future, so I must trust the information. As I process all the signs, synchronicities, and

spiritual downloads, I must discern the cost of not listening to myself.

Protecting Energy

Due to my personality, and perhaps because I think part of my life's purpose is attached to serving others, I attract all kinds of people with different energy fields (bright and dark). People with bright energy seldom leave you drained after engaging with them. These are the people who are in the moment, they laugh, tend to have a positive outlook on life, and there's a reciprocal exchange of energy with them. Is not that they are free from worries, and the concerns of the world, but they understand that in life there are highs and lows.

Conversely, people that carry dense or dark energy, usually stemming from unaddressed trauma, can leave you feeling weak, or tired after engaging with them. These people usually have a negative mindset, are problem focused rather than solution seeking, and hardly reciprocate. They are usually in need of an ear to emotionally disgorge their burdens.

As I began working on my energy, I began asking myself: What did it feel to be safe in my energy? How can I show up for others without depleting my energetic reservoir? For me, when I sense dark or dense energy, I begin praying internally as the person unpacks whatever situation they may be facing at the time, or if I know I must be around this person for a prolonged period.

Retreating from social interaction for a day allows me to replenish my energy. As much as possible, I go into nature after any exchange with someone who leaves me feeling depleted. If I'm helping people work through a difficult circumstance, I make sure to listen to music that uplifts me before or after speaking with that person.

I assess my body thoroughly to check for any energetic transference I might have picked up during that interaction so that I can transmute the energy.

Electrical companies will shut off sections of the power grid to avoid power outages and protect equipment and downtime whenever there's a peak demand in consumption. When my energy is "overactive" or used without a reservoir because I'm giving more time to addressing others' needs than mine, I will inevitably experience downtime (emotional fatigue).

The emotional downtime will manifest as exhaustion or sadness, depleting me of my natural ability to light up the internal grid that provides support to me and others.

I protect that grid by enforcing boundaries, knowing when to isolate to recharge, and doing things that bring joy into my life. Moreover, removing myself from people, places, and things that do not align with my energy or soul.

As I began to dive deep into my healing, I began working on all the wounds that had haunted me for so long. In my past, I had experienced deep betrayal from family, friends, and relationships. It was important to unpack those wounds for my self-preservation and future relationships, most importantly, the relationship with myself. Therefore, healing from that pain was necessary as I did not want to betray myself ever again.

I delved deep on the issue of "Impermanence" in my life. The programming that things do not last in my life- brought about from the wounds of loss, abuse, grief, and regret I carried.

I used to struggle with the fact that many of my relationships whether platonic, romantic, even professionally did not last. A strong bond would form, and then, vanish. I reconciled with the fact that nothing is permanent, not people, places, or things. The only permanence was the "experience" itself. The lesson learned. More importantly, when a cycle ends with friends, family, lovers, or a job, it has less to do with me, and more to do with how things are divinely orchestrated as every moment is connected. I know that every experience has led me to the next moment whether that's romantically, or professionally.

In doing the emotional work, I realized that I had raised my children with all the toxicity I garnered over my life. What I wanted most when I had my children was to raise them properly, and that at the very least they think of me as a "good and loving mother."

When I realized how my absenteeism from my own life, might have created unhealthy patterns for my children, I was beyond ashamed. My children who were the driving force of my life, I felt as though I damaged them. I was a provider, yes. I attended all the school plays, doctors' appointments, yes. I instilled values, and morals, yes. But my children witnessed the depressed mother. The over-worked mother. The mother who experienced all this abuse as I was raising them, and by default might not have been as emotionally present as I hoped to be. The mother who couldn't be fully present because I was always dealing with one problem after the other. The stressed mother. Although, I tried my best to hide it from them, children know. Children feel the absent mind of a parent. Children know when their mother is happy or not.

I felt guilty for the partners I chose as their fathers as that severely impacted them. Especially, for my son. I watched these men go and have a great life, vacation, buy anything they wanted, while I struggled financially while raising their children. More troublesome was drying their tears when their fathers didn't pick them up leaving them fully dressed, and for me to deal with their mess.

A part of me resented them, but mostly I resented me. Children need their fathers present. They need a male figure to guide them and let them know from a male's perspective how life works. I could only teach my children (especially my son) what a man should be like from my perspective. A female perspective.

I never forced their fathers to be financially responsible to their children (I regret that today), but I did expect them to

198

be there emotionally available for them. They reminded me
of my biological father. While I resented them but forgave
them years ago, I also know, that I would not have my
children without them.

Thankfully, Frank stepped in, and the "mother" in me
will be forever grateful to him for that.

In Latino culture, parents do not feel obliged to ask
children for forgiveness for the generational trauma(s)
passed on to their children. For the abuse, and or neglect,
because so long as the children were provided for, clothed,
and fed is considered sufficient. But children need love.
Affection is a requirement. Conversations about how to
navigate life is what shapes children who become healthy
adults. To have their feelings acknowledge. To be able to
sleep in their parent's bed if they had a nightmare.

I asked my children forgiveness for bringing them up
with all the trauma I carried. I asked for forgiveness for all
the generational trauma I knowingly or unknowingly passed
on to them. For the poor choices I made that might have
caused them pain. For not being there, or more present as I
was navigating life while raising them.

I began working on the areas where they felt I came
short. I think my children know that I have always been their
advocate. Once they got older, it was easier to divulge my
past to them. And because I have two amazing human beings
who are full of life, filled with empathy, and a knowing that
we are all on this earth to evolve our soul, they forgave me...,
at least for some of my transgressions.

I have sought to have a closeness with my children,
perhaps the closeness that I could not achieve with my
parents. I could not get that closeness with my children
without first admitting that I did not know anything about
raising children but did try my best. I had to set my parental
pride aside and humble myself before them.

Disclaimer: I am still working on it.

Deo Volente "God willing"
(The last letter to my children)

Deo Volente
Life will always smile at you,
may your garden's soil be moistened,
may your trees give fruits and your
harvest be forever sacred.

Deo Volente
Your heart be filled with rhymes,
Verses to position you to expect the most beautiful life.
May your mouth compose poetic kisses
And may you always
Keep your soul clean and peaceful.

Deo Volente
The world will be your accomplice,
Linking itself to your life, the way
a newborn attaches to its mother's bosom,
to be nurtured through each stage of life.

Deo Volente
May you dance in the rain without fear of getting wet.
May the wind always breathe relief to your inlands.
I hope you understand,
that enduring painful bursts..., it's also a part of life!
I pray that when you walk through such a moment, you take
a deep breath, resting assure that it's just a strong draft, and
as such,
it too shall pass.
I hope you love to explore the Earth,
May you be fascinated by its forests, mountains, valleys, and
hills.
Did you know? One learns much by sauntering through its
majestic ruins.

Deo Volente,
You marvel at the sight of a bridge,
Giving you insight on how relationships are built.

Deo volente
Music becomes your best friend,
Find refuge in its lyrics and melodies as well.
May they fill you with harmony, joy, and strength.
Keep smiling even in the worst of nightmares.
Be kind to the indigent and always remember,
That one day, you too, may need compassion, as well.

Love freely as night and day,
May your heart never experience need or demand.
If a person doesn't love you…, bless them and go your way.
The right person will eventually come,
one who shall value and love you till the end of times.
Keep this piece of advice:
To attract love,
you must first be benevolent and love yourself.

It's almost time to go and for an indefinite time,
I will have to leave you behind. Remember that I've always
prayed for you, and you are my best work of art.

Deo Volente
We will meet once again at the cyclical point
where everything revolves.
From afar, I will guide your steps,
please keep to my advice.
See you soon and remember,
You are my '**capolavoro**'.
While you may not see me for some time,
You will forever be...my beautiful little child.

Five

As I began integrating and unlearning all the programming and old belief systems, I ascertained that I had to make peace with the parts of me that felt abandoned by my father.

My biological father had been in and out most of my life. Ironically enough, of all his children, I was closest to him, and everyone would say I was the "apple of his eyes". I think he was closest to me because I physically reminded him of my mother.

Of all my mother's attributes, I think her grace and kindness have shaped how I see the world. My mother had all the right to do what many women in toxic relationships do..., *weaponize their children*. My mother is made from a different fabric.

My mother's relationship with my paternal side of the family is nothing short of admirable. She did a great job at keeping us close with my paternal side of the family. Some of my greatest childhood memories were spent visiting Haverstraw, a town located in Central New York where my father and his relatives lived, and many Dominican immigrants from the north of the country migrated to in the 70's and 80's. I spent many holidays with them; they were lively, funny, familial, joyful, and fun.

My father was a good-looking man, impeccably dressed and funny, and one of those Dominicans that we he drank his English was more deducible than his Spanish. He drank a lot. He loved to take pictures and when he drank, one of his idioms was "Let's take a picture for the photo I.D," whatever that meant.

My biological father was not present in the way that many dads are. He did not call my house (don't think he was allowed). He didn't show up with Christmas gifts, or call on birthdays, but whenever me and my siblings went to visit Haverstraw, he would resuscitate from whatever hole he was in and made his way to see us. I surmise that he was proud of his children (whom he did not support financially, emotionally, or otherwise). He would galvanize his friends to introduce them to us. He was proud that my mother and stepdad raised us well. Perhaps it was melancholy or shame for not being there. But I know that when my father saw me, his eyes lit up. He had these beautiful big dark eyes—soul penetrating. Deeply saddened. Nevertheless, you could see galaxies in his irises when he saw me, or any of my siblings.

Perchance, I was closest to him because I was a Capricorn like him. Perhaps, it is because I like talking to people and getting to know them deeply. Perhaps, because of all his children, I was the most gullible. I don't know. I know that he always took time to speak with me. He hugged me long and hard. Even when he was harsh in speech, he would immediately apologize to me.

When he got sick, he'd been trying to be more consistent in my life and getting a cancer diagnosis moved him even closer. There is nothing like the Angel of Death to make you reconsider what is important. I accompanied him to some appointments and followed up with his healthcare team. He succumbed to cancer a few days before my 40th birthday, and following my father's death, it was as if my entire life was revealed to me.

My favorite number has always been five, which is also my Science Project's favorite number. My father's birthday was on the 5th. I was molested at the age of five. It took five years for me to reunite with my mother, and every five years, I go through enormous transformations.

In spiritual numerology, five is the call to change. A universal push that forces change in a situation or a person.

My father's death left a profound pain in me because I felt robbed of more time with him. He was far from perfect, but he was trying to right his wrongs. Death does that. It's almost as if, with his passing, the part of me that longed for him all my life finally found peace.

I began noticing the patterns in my love life. Most of these men were my father in some way. They avoided responsibility for themselves, and others while giving all their attention to their friends, their work, their vices, women, etc.

I began losing fear over everything. Almost as if my father's death gave me permission to live more freely. I believe "forgiveness" did that. There was a peace of mind in me when my father passed perhaps, because I was there for him until his last days. That forgiveness released a part of my childhood I contended with for so long.

By the time of his death, I saw him as a man who made mistakes, flawed, but also a man who was deeply saddened, and who had childhood traumas as well. Traumas he didn't get to address. But I also saw the man he wished he could have been all along. A man with a family. He got to see, hug, kiss, and laugh with his grandchildren. Sit at my table to enjoy a lunch or a dinner. Have regular phone or in person conversations about what life is and is not. About regrets, dreams lost, and lots of jokes.

After my father's passing, creativity sparked again. A creativity that had been stalled for years after Frank commented about my writing abilities which instilled serious doubts in me about ever being published. But when my father died, writing was the only outlet that helped me transmute that grief.

I began writing poetry consistently and sharing my work on Facebook as I lost the fear of sharing my talent. Writing has always been a way for me to process and release my inner turmoil. It also allows me to reclaim parts of me. I did not see my writing as a talent or a gift, nor did I think anyone would be interested in reading them. It was mine. Nevertheless, I got some notoriety in the digital poetry community and two years later, a publishing house in Spain asked me to join an International Poetry contest birthing my first book, *Entre el Amor Y Otras Cosas del Destino,* which was published in 2018. The English version was translated that same year under the title, *Of Love and other Matters of Fate.*

I remembered Frank's words and thought to myself - Happy chaos!

Biblically, the number five means: God's grace, goodness and favor. As I pondered on the process, and what my father's death meant for me, I understood how God's grace, goodness and favor have always followed me. I remind myself of this grace when I think of unfavorable things. That there's grace in transformation. There's goodness in allowing the old things to wither away whether that's patterns of thinking, behavior that is no longer aligned with your destiny. Pain that no longer serve to fuel the journey. I can see the favor in my life. In the experiences I've lived. The people I have met along the way.

I began to understand the journey more profoundly. The more I thought about my father, who he was and wasn't in my life, the more life revealed itself to me, metaphysically starting the biggest journey of all.

The journey to UNLOVING ME.

Almond Eyes

A girl with almond eyes is missing,
She has shiny-silky skin,
with dimples on her countenance,
And her smile is like the first joyful day of spring.

A girl with a white embroidered dress has gone missing,
Knitted by pricked hands with the light off.
She wears a headband that announces hope, containing all
the stories I told her before bed.
I don't know if you have ever lost something,
-But if you find her, could you call me?

Looking for a girl with the aroma of sunrise,
I don't know where I've lost her,
perhaps, as I stretched my arms!
She looked north with fear and reluctance,
suddenly, her hands slipped away, as I raised mine to praise.

A girl with almond eyes is missing.
She can barely run, barely speak,
barely thinks...

Amidst sorrows my peace shrunk,
traversing the face of the earth looking for her without a
trace.
Her face is imprinted in my anguished and condemned soul.

A girl with almond eyes is missing,
She has disappeared without a trace,
The only clue is the light her eyes emit.
Perhaps, I lost her in El Malecon Del Sur,
or in any icy New York City Street.

I am looking for a little girl with a mole on her cheek,
with cheekbones that inflate between smiles and laughter,
mine have deflated between bloody weeping,

206

while the seconds pass without being able to find her.

I am not a bad mother.
No, please don't point your fingers,
I closed my eyes to clear my vision,
and when I opened them
- my little girl had gone missing.

She wears two silver bracelets on her wrists:
One is engraved and the other has a compass
hiding her home address.

I don't know if you understand my plight,
but, in case you see her lost in the crowd,
in case you recognize her light
know it's my almond-eyed girl,
she is my 'Blue Unicorn',
and my bright shining North-Star!

To five-year-old me
I Love and admire you.

The Journey to Soul-Me
I Didn't Let It Go to Shit

The beginning of the Covid-19 pandemic was terrifying for humanity. Nevertheless, it provided much-needed soul respite in a morbid way for all. The imposed lockdown gave me "time" for the first time in my life. I had been feeling exhausted for quite some time. It wasn't only physical exhaustion. My soul felt tired. I was anxiously at peace, yet discontent.

I had been resisting change and rest for a very long time. You either take care of yourself, or life will take care of it for you. In the months leading to the pandemic, I had been experiencing severe body swelling and rapid weight gain despite working out daily and having a healthy diet.

I was experiencing a kind of fatigue that was terrifying me, yet there was nothing in my medical labs indicating any illness. As one Specialist put it: "Labs are normal, but there's something brewing" (Thanks for nothing Einstein, it was the brewing that brought me here, I thought). The American healthcare system never seems to surprise me.

The labs coming back normal signaled to me that another spiritual awakening was soon approaching.

The uncertainty and massive loss of life were beginning to affect me emotionally. I began experiencing severe sadness, and all the issues I had been working on for years, and foolishly thought I had healed from began bubbling up. The thing about healing is that it's a never-ending journey.

Due to the instability in my childhood, one of the things I have feared most in life is the lack of stability. I have dealt with financial limitations in the past, but having a source of income assured me that I would overcome- that I could always curtail spending to live within my means. This time was different. I had no source of income, and the stability I worked for all my life was crumbling before my eyes, heightening my anxiety about the future.

Every door was locked, and despite my best efforts, I could not find employment. It was infuriating that with my experience and education, I could not find work, and anything I attempted to generate an income with did not yield fruit during that period. I felt as though I was blacklisted from the universe.

God told me to rest. I resisted. God told me again to rest; I asked God to send me another sign. God yelled, "REST," and I kept questioning him- how would I be able to provide for and survive without employment? As more doors kept closing and my anxiety deepening, I surrendered to God's plan.

I had been living in survival mode my whole life, working myself to exhaustion because even when I had living partners, I was financially responsible for the household. If the relationship didn't work, I did not need to rely on their income to survive. On the surface, it was this awareness about my hyper-independence. On a deeper level, God tested whether I trusted him enough to go through it. To surrender to his plan. To give it all up for my healing.

I have seen God's hand in every phase of my life. I saw him when I had two car accidents, feeling as though supernatural forces lifted me out of those cars, which could have ended catastrophically for me. Through that horrendous night my ex-boyfriend raped me. Through suicide attempts, molestation, and all the other challenges I have experienced. This type of surrender was different. He was demanding that I leave everything behind. I unquestioningly upheld his command.

God was dealing with my existence. The same existence I had been 'just' managing as if he did not deposit greatness in me. As if he did not give me dreams and desires. As if "responsibility" was the only adjective that defined me (Why make me a Capricorn if responsibility did not define me?).

I integrated many lessons that helped me release most of my past. I exercised and enforced boundaries across all areas of my life (family, friends, etc.) I released every relationship that created unnecessary turmoil in my life. I began prioritizing my mental health by not engaging in "people-pleasing" behavior and said NO to things I did not want to engage with. I was empowered.

Pressing forward, one step before the other, has been my mantra in powering through life. Working gave me the financial freedom and ability to never be susceptible or stay bound to anyone if I wanted to leave. I was at the mercy of God and the universe. I didn't understand that my inner child had been yelling for respite. This was God's way of returning me to my inner child. That frightful little girl wanted to be taken care of, to have fun, to finally be free from the bondage I had imprisoned her in.

The strangest things began happening. I began to see three-year-old me, five-year-old me, and even teenage-year-old me in random New York City streets. I once saw my shadow on the pavement as I was walking home. Instead of seeing my shadow, I saw adult me and a smaller shadow holding my hand (I thought for sure this was going to land me in the Psych ward for longer than three weeks).

Initially, I did not understand why I kept seeing different versions of myself in the streets. Or seeing vivid images of my younger self in different places I had been in my past.

During that time, I was spending a lot of time by the Hudson River and the Inwood Hill trails. This was where I went to meditate, since I had time. And as I began communing more and more with nature, it was apparent why these visions, and shadows were regurgitating back up to the surface. I needed to peel back another layer of my journey.

The synchronicities and the spiritual downloads or messages I received during this period got louder and louder. I understood the chirping of birds. Nature spoke to me in every way. My ancestors spoke to me daily. I cried (a lot), laughed, and panicked because I was unemployed. I had no source of income but was traveling every few months. I would think of travel, and someone would gift me a plane ticket. I lacked for nothing during this time (not food, shelter, entertainment, etc.) Family and friends supported me in ways that I could never repay.

It was uncomfortable. I was grateful for all the financial, emotional, and spiritual support I was receiving, but the person I grew into being was uncomfortable during this period. I don't know how to ask for help. Receiving help always came at a price for me, and being at the mercy of needing people shook the very foundation I built (trauma built). I was uncomfortable with being still. Initially I embraced the stillness, but uncertainty was calling me.

Hiking trails are so revealing if one pays close attention. Unbeknownst to me, as I walked through the only forest in Manhattan, absorbing, and observing all the glory and history that is embedded in the Inwood Hills trails, the terrain was revealing to me: that just like this beautiful landscape covered in glacial potholes and cottonwood trees, I too had to unearth what these visions were about.

I held on to the version of me that produced and provided, and was always so busy for so long, that it shook me to my core to face my biggest fear: "Stability" and "uncertainty" were commanding a hearing from those earlier wounded versions of me.

But God! God was telling me that I would always be provided for. I am not a job. I am not just a provider. That I don't just exist. Through observing nature, God was revealing to me how even in destruction there's a process of restoration. That the muck, the mud, and the manure enrich the soil. He was reconnecting me back to legacy rather than success.
That I was already a success because I existed and persisted.

Almost as a reminder, the first job I got after three years of a "universal blacklist" the journey would land me between Worth and Pearl Street. God is funny that way. I have always loved pearls, and many in the poetry community dubbed me as "The Black Pearl of the Caribbean." A reminder that like a pearl – I am one in several million, and to always remember my Worth!

I didn't let anything go to shit. I was right on track with life's timing. The process of becoming has as much to do with surrender as it does with taking charge when need be. That is okay to rest, to enjoy life. To enjoy your success, as well as your failures. Failures are an asset to achieving joy because the understanding that all moments are connected is the greatest lesson one can learn.

Had it not been for what I perceived as unfortunate events in my life, I wouldn't have acquired the wisdom to help people in their time of pain, need, or loss. My life has prepared me, be it through the fire, through painful losses, and or experiences.

I have come to accept that life is not linear. That joy is everlasting because it is a state of being. That happiness is fleeting, and that *love is the most powerful force an individual can harness for and from themselves and others.* Through my very existence, I have freed myself and, hopefully, others as well. I broke free from the bondage of trauma by going through it. By dissecting it layer by layer.

Accepting that five was a call to change, to evolution, connecting me to my higher self, and heed that call. Applying the lessons learned, understanding the psychology of my trauma, and how I managed and processed emotions, helped me modify my behavior. Trauma, nor your feelings can be intellectualized. To heal it you must: Sit in it, be with it, smell it; Ask it: What does it need to heal? Why does it hurt? Why does it want to stay? What can it morph into?

Healing must include the elements of psychology and spiritual integration simultaneously. The latter is the agent of transmutation (utilizing pain, energy, and emotion to create something beautiful and new with it.)

For me, connection to spirit, a spiritual practice, allowed for the alchemizing of those events, emotions, and trauma. I transmuted through my poetry, writing, service to others, and other creative outlets.

While the brightness of my innocence made its roots at the bottom of the swamp, I emerged as the most beautiful lotus flower.

The experiences I lived, and the abuse I endured were the root in the mud. But the wisdom I amassed became the stems by which I navigated my life; finally reaching the top by integrating the lessons learned. All the experiences, my children, the hope I gave myself, and the faith I found through God were the lengthy stems reaching upward to find the top of the water.

There at the top, the lush blossoms grew (tenacity, consciousness,) and as I blossomed, the blooms unfolded one by one. Petal by petal (learning to love all of me,) emerging immaculate from the murky water (pain).

All lotuses have a protective outer coating that repels the dirt and water. Through spirituality and developing gratitude for the journey I was able ward off the dirt that abuse left in me and use the water as cleansing mechanism to keep my spirit clean.

The petals of my integrity returned as I found purity within my heart. I struggled to see purity or divinity within me because I felt tainted from such an early age. I struggled to accept that dirt washes away. My past, and my decisions which mostly came from a place of wound met me with incessant derision.

As I began to immerse myself spiritually, my soul began revealing how I was still pure. That what made me pure was not the physical violation of my soul, rather, that no person can take purity or divinity from me because is inherently mine; my purity is embedded in my divine organism. Moreover, that what made me pure was my willingness only to change and to use my own life as a service to others that are in pain. To love people past their perceived realities.

I released love into the ether, and the universe showered me with loving rain. I used that rain (tears from painful experiences) to water and wash myself of all the beliefs systems that told me I wasn't pure, or worthy.

The water moisturized the humidity of past heartbreaks, distorted thinking of self; and to plant a love tree rooted in faith, in love of self. I pushed all that love back out into the universe, and that love is continuously boomeranging back to me.

My eyes found moons they could rely on, and my sun-kissed lips which once shivered in fear, found freedom in the voice I had suppressed for so long, and I now speak freely and with authenticity.

My skin found nourishment in the knowing of Who I Am, and after I slept with fear for an entire lifetime, I befriended it, giving it the light it needed to bring *hope* to the center stage of my life.

Little One
(we grew up)

Hello little one!
Oh, how I've missed you.
I want to catch up with you, do you have a minute?
We are now 44, I know, you must think I'm so old!
We have two beautiful children,
and a star for a grandchild!
Life has been beautifully chaotic for us,
But we have also had lots of fun.

We have gone through a lot of stuff.
Lots of pain, betrayal, and unfortunately more abuse.
But we have also experienced a lot of love, lots of expansion,
lots of growth.
You grow up to be kind, smart, funny, beautiful, and fun.
We are an ear to many, just like you when we were small.

You became a poet and writer, and so much more.
No, we did not become a lawyer, but we seek justice for all.
We still have time to fulfill that dream,
later, I will let you know.
You became comfort for so many.
You are deeply loved.

I want to thank you for being so strong,
your bravery and your soul.
You endured so much and kept a smile on (we still do that).
You don't need to be afraid anymore.
I went back in time and rescued you from Cuco el Abusador.
We grew up now and know how to say NO.
Sadly, it happened to us once more at 24,
but, because of your strength, I got through it all.

I have spent a lifetime searching for love,
trying to heal the wounds of abandonment, of abuse and
control.

215

That caused me to look for love in all the wrong places,
and as a result, has caused lots of wounds.

Remember how close we were with God? We still are.
I have gone on an infinite spiritual journey to heal us from
our past.
In that process we found self-love which is the best kind.
We now do things that are good for us.
We love ourselves so much,
when we enter a room, the room lights up
(we've always had that)
because we became whole. Yes, you and I, became one.

I want to thank you for all you taught me.
I want to thank for staying positive.
I want to thank you for loving me so much.
I love and have the highest admiration for you, little one.
I started standing in the rain the way you used to, and it
brings me so much joy.
We still sing a lot, and look up at the night sky, the moon,
and the stars.

I Got My Shit Back

Minister Joyce Myer always says: "Life can only be understood backward." The lockdown gave me a balcony perspective on my journey, so, I decided to go back to Soul School and get a Ph.D. (Philosophizing, Humanizing, and re-Designing) Me.

My journey is all about love. For years I contended with God about why did I really need to go through betrayal, abuse, volatile relationships, and the trauma I amassed over my life.

Those relationships taught me about fellowship and communing with myself. Every single one of those men, revealed another layer within me, that placed the responsibility on me to change what was and not acceptable in my life. Perhaps, I struggled to leave at an earlier stage in relationships because I lacked clarity and awareness around what is purposeful in a relationship, and what is vexing to my soul. Nevertheless, I always allowed myself room to make tough decisions despite breaking my own heart, and eventually left them.

Every single one of those men saw *power* in me, and that I was a force to be reckoned with. Instead, of "receiving" my love, and my power as an asset, they demeaned, belittled, manipulated, and abused me to get me to shrink, to get me to submission because is the only way they could ever keep me close. Nevertheless, my spirit never allowed me to fully submit.

I never had "what's a good man" conversation with any adult as I was growing up. I had what "women need to do" to keep a house going conversation. I am not clear where I knew that it wasn't acceptable to accept betrayal to keep a relationship, or accept misery, and feeling depleted of one's life force to feel loved. Innately, I knew that was not what I wanted for my life.

Those relationships were catalysts for me to choose me every single time. To desire better for me. To love me in

217

the way God loves me. To love me delicately. To prioritize my needs, my desires, my gifts, and my destiny.

While the journey was about love, it was never about romantic love or loving any man! Instead, my life was about going through what seemed like insurmountable challenges at the time; sorrows, all the happy chaos I endured - to fall in love with my story.

To fall in love with three-year-old me, who at such a young age understood responsibility, and applied that wisdom to navigate through life with a keen understanding that we are all responsible for each other.

The little girl who felt abandoned by life and fell in love with the parts of my abandonment issues, and the acceptance that my parents (Mother and Stepdad) did the absolute best they could while managing their own pain, trauma, and journey. I understood that I grew up in a time when addressing traumas became more viable and acceptable across society, but that was not the case for my parents.

Nevertheless, the responsibility to address, and fully understand me (my triggers, my pain, my fears, et. cetera) fell solely on me. I understood that I wanted a different emotionally enriched life for myself; therefore, doing the emotional and spiritual work was a commandment for me.

I know my mother did not abandon me. As with most immigrants, she was forced to leave me back home to ensure a better future. I understood this ages ago. She left me in the care of people she felt were responsible. However unfortunate the events that unfolded because of her leaving, I know I come from a loving, kind, fun, generous, supportive family (all trees have some rotten fruit.)

I have amazing, loving, kind siblings whose love and support have enriched my life. A mother whose sacrifice made it possible for an entire family to extend their wings beyond El Mar Caribe.

I come from a lineage of powerful, strong, diligent, courageous, and fearless women who carried on their backs an entire village. I come from my abuela Juana's softness and

218

my Mama Nena's sternness. From the humbleness and love of my Papa Melanio.

I often caution people in the healing journey with some of the "New Age Spirituality" concepts, especially the notion that you must dissociate and abandon everyone in your lineage to heal. In my opinion, this type of messaging is toxic and divisive, and its only intent is to deepen the divide among family and friends. We all have baggage. We all have trauma (some of us more than others,) but we all have shadows to work through. Dissociating from everyone is what has this world feeling so disconnected, depressed, and lonely.

Healing is about addressing the unhealed parts within, taking accountability, and holding yourself and people accountable. Yes, we must distance ourselves from people who are vexing to our souls. However, that differs from the narrative that everyone goes into the "perpetrator's bucket."

Shadow work requires an honest conversation with self and God (Source, Gaia, or whatever energy you believe in). Shadow work is an investigative process into the self, the past, and the unknown, aligning those aspects to balance the present and future. Shadow work creates boundaries, and boundaries are different from dissociation.

My journey helped me fall in love with five-year-old me, who was molested and, as a result, became scared of nightfall, only to fall in love with the moon. It was to find solace in the darkest and deepest wounds to address my shadows and shine a light on the generational dysfunctions within my family.

It was necessary to pull the rug as uncomfortable as it was and vacuum the issues haunting the ancestral line. More importantly, that I was not responsible for healing s/he who did not deem it appropriate. I was not responsible for carrying that weight on my shoulders because it was like holding water in my hands, it would run through my fingers.

The journey was to fall in love with the frightened eighteen-year-old single parent who struggled to raise her children. Who constantly worried if she would be able to protect them from harm? If she could guide and instill values that would help them become their authentic selves, while being productive members of society. To fall in love with all the shameful and guilty parts that come from not knowing what you are doing as a parent.

The journey was about finding the space to pour back into myself the love I sought out externally, and so willingly gave to others before asking myself: Leydis Diana, do you have a reserve for you?

I fell in love with the love stories that taught me about myself and boundaries, in turn, pushing me towards every spiritual awakening I have undergone. All those men taught me who I am and who I am not. They taught me that *indifference* is not a plate I want to eat from because I deserve reciprocity, respect, love, and gentleness. They taught me that I have an immense capacity to love, and that I do not need to tolerate insufferable, noxious, or disrespectful situations to deserve love. They taught about forgiveness.

My journey made me fall in love with my sensitivity, which I reneged so much of. I understood that my sensitivity was not a curse but a gift, granting me the ability to connect to others in a real and authentic way.

My sensitivity was a bridge to help others navigate through their own challenges, and pain, vicariously healing mine. That while unfortunate, my experiences provided me a plethora of relatability to almost everyone I encounter.

Unbeknownst to me, that range of experiences is what positioned me to make their souls feel safe to share their stories despite me being a stranger to many of them. That sensitivity I reneged of, allowed me to teach or offer people a different perspective of perceiving their pain. To pull from them the lessons they could draw from, what those lessons were trying to teach them about themselves, and their

220

self-love. It helped to bring them closer to spirituality, not founded in religion, but in a personal relationship with God.

My pain seeded my purpose because not only did it give me resilience, and a different way of viewing and resolving problems, but it also empowered me every time I overcame a challenge in my life. It strengthened my emotional and spiritual countenance. Pain taught me how to care for others, and to advocate for those who could not speak or defend themselves.

Earlier in the text, I spoke about "Saviors Complex" which I thought is what I was doing. But it isn't. I am not trying to "save anyone," I am trying to help those going through pain to see the beauty within themselves. To let them know that their pain is their teacher, a trampoline to a version of themselves that is free, and unattached. That they deserve to know how much beauty they possess despite their perceived "brokenness." It is gut wrenching to see people suffer. Defeated by life. So many people don't know where to begin to heal. I serve as a bridge to explore their pain; God does the rest.

The Russian novelist Fyodor Dostoevsky, wrote in his novel Crime and Punishment: "The darker the night, the brighter the stars..., the deeper the grief the closer to God."

This quote helps me to reflect on the kind of world we are morphing into. Perhaps, it has always been this way. A society driven by selfishness, self-centeredness, and exploitation of the weak. When did we become so comfortable watching people suffer?

I know what it took to heal me. To remove out of my physical, emotional, and spiritual vortex the density that abuse, and betrayal embossed in me. The many layers that I had to peel off to reveal me. The real me. Therefore, I will not leave those suffering on their own if I can assist, and if they ask for help. We can all share a resource, a phone number, make a call, listen to someone, hug, et cetera. That is the mandate - love. ***Every time a person heals, heaven sings.***

The journey was about recognizing the parts of me that were wounded and healing them - for me! That my wounds were not ugly and did not make me "unlovable." That I was not my wounds, but rather, that I did not succumb to the darkness I endured. To the contrary, I fused it with my internal light to peacefully coexist.

The path was never about loving a man but falling in love with the different tunes I have played in my own songs. The inspired verse of my poetry.

I know that the sprint in my step is purposeful as I walk through the streets of my beloved Washington Heights. These Washington Heights streets that loaned its pavements to a child full of fears. Who provided its beautiful landscape for her tears to fall onto. This beautiful community gave me unlimited opportunities for growth, and inspired action. These "Heights" housed all the stories of what love would be and would not.

I have managed to survive, excel, and thrive despite the fear or obstacles. This woman born in La Feria, Santo Domingo, proudly raised in Washington Heights - transformed herself, as did the neighborhood. I Am Heights, and the Heights is me, even if camouflaged under the decor of change (gentrification), for me (healing).

I fell in love with the courage it took to allow all the versions of me to die to birth a new me. The commitment to growth, to the evolution of thought, whether emotional or spiritual, as part of my ascension process. To become a woman who realizes her dreams one at a time, and to understand that I still have time on my side.

The journey was about forgiving me. To fall in love with the journey of "Unloving" what trauma tried to imprint in me, and "Loving" myself back to soul-me.

That I Am my Soul's Mate. That I Am Love.

That love is me…

And

that is a beautiful discovery,

and

the best love story I can give myself.

I Am

I am the roses no one gave me,
I am the lover of all the verses ever written about love.
To jazz, I am its trumpet,
and the first song ever sung.

I am the dream that was not deferred.
I am the opportunities that were rejected,
but found purpose instead.
To purpose, I am its mission.

I am the answer to longing.
I am the slow tingling, both hands in your face,
butterflies before a kiss.

I am the path filled with ancient trees that murmur…
Change is coming! Change is here. Change is me.

I am the sound of hope.
I am the courage that withstood rejection,
rejection, ejecting me into realms
where violence and non-resistance meet.
I resisted, persisted, and shifted the trajectory
of the many while sacrificing my own.

I am the wisdom of my ancestors yelling
"sigue mi hija, que ya te hicimos camino."
I am what my ancestors didn't think was possible.

I am the agreement in discord.
I am the truth in controversy.
I am the hips that glide in strength.
I am the stretch mark to those who have been stretched.

I am the company of the lonely.
I am the spirit that walks before your step.
I am the ears to the deaf.

I step into universes filled with laughter, joy, and peace,
to reveal it to everyone I meet.

I am the rhythm that dances with the future.
I am what war is afraid of.
I am the revelation of character.
I am a sight to the blind.

I am the twist in the plot.

I am.

I was.

I'm still becoming.

The End
Impossible…Life continues)

Thank you for staying this long (You are brave!)
May your journey be blessed, joyful, hopeful, generous,
kind, fulfilling, and loving.

I Love You.

Acknowledgments

As I conclude this book, an enormous sense of peace and gratitude fills up my soul.

I dedicated this book to God, because he has been my anchor, and source of strength throughout my journey. He has been my friend, my confidant, and healer.

I remember the first time he whispered, "Write your story." I didn't think much of my story at the time as I heard him say this. One day, in 2007 amid one of the biggest heartbreaks, I sat in my children's room, and began writing the stories compiled in this book. I couldn't finish it then because it pained and triggered me every time, I sat down to edit the book. But God has not allowed me to rest about completing this book, and as life kept taking place, I kept delaying its completion.

I want to give God the glory and grace for all the help he has provided, and all the people he has sent into my life who have transformed my human evolution.

I cannot explain the immense gratitude I have for everyone who has been part of my journey.

To my children and my beautiful grandchild who are the most beautiful reflection of love in human form. Thank you for existing, and giving me purpose, teaching me, growing me, loving me, and yes, challenging me.

To my beautiful family and friends who have loved and supported all the versions of me. My life is better because you are in it.

To all the strangers that were earth angels in a chapter of my story, thank you, your kindness has never left me.

Neisha Feliciano, our meeting was fated somewhere in the stars. Thank you for coming into my life.

I want to thank Dr. Diana Hernandez for editing my book.

Thank you ©2024 BojanR@pixelstudio for this beautiful cover which I am so in love with.

Brian J. Segarra, thank you for the fabulous photoshoots, which would make the cover. Our conversations about the journey, and the way God works have been nothing but awe inspiring.

Leydis D. De La Cruz is a bilingual writer-poet, born in the Dominican Republic, raised in Washington Heights, New York City. Her first book *Entre El Amor Y Otras Cosas Del Destino* was published in 2018 under the pseudo-name, LeydisProse. The book was later translated into English under the title *Of Love and Other Matters of Fate*. Her second book *Unloving Me: A Memoir of a Girl from The Heights* was published in 2024.

Made in the USA
Middletown, DE
22 August 2024